D0513912

THE SMALLHOLDER'S GUIDE

THE SMALLHOLDER'S GUIDE

C J MUNROE

with an Introduction by Ian Niall

David & Charles

Newton Abbot   London   North Pomfret(Vt)

British Library Cataloguing in Publication Data

Munroe, C J
   The smallholder's guide.
   1. Agriculture
   I. Title
   630   S521

ISBN 0–7153–7652–7

Library of Congress Catalog Card Number 78–74077

Photoset and printed in Great Britain
by Redwood Burn Limited Trowbridge and Esher.
for David & Charles (Publishers) Limited
Brunel House Newton Abbot Devon

Published in the United States of America
by David & Charles Inc
North Pomfret   Vermont 05053   USA

CONTENTS

Drawings by Denys Baker
Photograph on p 19, courtesy J. Allan Cash;
all other photographs courtesy John Topham Picture
Library

INTRODUCTION

The harsh truth about many smallholdings is that the owner or tenant discovers that there is invariably too much to do for one man while enlisting help will mean starvation for two. At the same time agricultural experts frighten even the man who goes in for things in a bigger way by telling him that on a certain acreage of land there isn't a living to be made. The small farm is 'uneconomic'. Costings prove this. Yields per acre are easily worked out.

Agriculture is a science as well as an art. A man who farms on any scale cannot simply pretend that his way holds the answer, when an outsider can estimate his wages bill, his depreciation, his investment return on so many items in mixed farming. Even big farmers can become vulnerable because of their heavy investment in special equipment, or because they put all their eggs in one basket. The small farmer can never raise enough money to do what he wants to do and make a living. He hardly dares include his wages.

Outside the realm of farming proper are a great many small men who do not call themselves farmers. No one covets their acreage, except perhaps the builder who wants to put up houses and exploit the housing shortage by speculating. Land is, of course, scheduled and the smallholder is as secure in his tenancy as he can ever hope to be, but his way of life is one of the hardest there is. To survive on land that will hardly yield good grass, or grow a crop to improve a modest bank balance between one season and the next, takes a very special tenacity and a capacity to operate the swings and roundabouts that even the small farmer with twenty cows and a fair acreage of arable may not be able to employ.

Nevertheless, the dedicated smallholder is there, sometimes holding on by his fingertips, working hours no one else would ever work, as obstinate as the pig he backs into a crate with a bucket over its head!

I must admit that I haven't the courage to go it alone on a holding, although there was a time when I might have asked to have my land registered as one, with the blessing of the district valuer. The proposition that my four acres (there are holdings smaller, believe it or not) might come within the scope of the law governing holdings was never put before anyone, for my enthusiasm died almost the moment it flourished. The Inland Revenue might just have blessed me but they would have asked me to keep books. There would have to have been a duly audited profit-and-loss reckoning to go before the inspector.

It wasn't just an aversion to the awful tedium of clerical transactions that put me off. Wealth cannot be created out of paperwork. When it comes down to it there is a Marxian truth that the first investment is labour. Thereafter there is organization, routine and planning. I shirked the responsibility of running my small patch on such organized lines that I dared not take a holiday, or leave the beans unpicked, to become a loss, or the rows unweeded to diminish my return. A smallholding doesn't look after itself. Not only has there to be order and daily labour to maintain a standard, there also has to be discipline of a kind inherent in successful husbandry. There is a time for sowing and planting and a time for gathering in, and neither can be put off. I hadn't the heart for it because I wasn't born to it, country-reared though I am. Deep within me was the knowledge that no one plays at being a smallholder if he expects reward for his enterprise. There is never a pot of gold at the end of it. A bank manager will not allow his smallholder customer to wax euphoric about his prospects, and even if he does he won't lend him any large sum of money. What little loan he offers will be backed by hard labour for there isn't much of an asset upon which the bank can foreclose.

I wasn't in this situation of course, and didn't need to make a living from my bit of orchard, pasture, kitchen garden and jungle beyond my wood. No, I said, when my accountant talked about how I was managing my affairs, however well it might sound on paper, I must face up to the fact that I have no lasting enthusiasm for the hoe, the spade, or for the endless chores of cultivating more than I might consume at my own table.

I had the dream, however. I considered what I might have done by going in for things commercially. I considered goats, or at least one goat which might be tethered on the scrub. Supposing this goat didn't browse on the yew, which is poisonous to cows. Supposing it munched happily on thorn and bramble and even reduced the jungle, would it be efficient as a milk-producing animal on such poor fare? I doubted whether a self-respecting goatkeeper would ask to tether his goat on my land for free, but there was another hurdle. Given that I kept a goat and milk resulted, for I had no thought of keeping a billy, I would surely have much more milk than we could consume and what to do with the milk? I could make cheese or yoghurt; but there would be the problem of selling cheese and yoghurt, and I had no idea of the market or of the lengths I might have to go to to sell what I produced. I turned away from the dream of keeping goats in the old orchard, where they would browse on better grass and only once in a while nibble at the bark of the old tree or the young shoots within reach. I dismissed the scheme when I thought about the stint at the milking platform, and all that fuss controlling temperature to make curd or keep a yoghurt culture going. If such things are really no problem to the person who wants to do them, they nevertheless killed off my goatkeeping schemes before they ever got beyond the dream.

I thought of growing mushrooms; I had the right place for

it and concrete boxes in which to keep the compost primed with the spore. I went from this to other dreams, such as using the greenhouses to grow grapes, hundredweights of tomatoes, masses of chrysanthemums. There always seemed to be difficulties before anything got off the ground. The cold-house grape never comes on well enough to have the high sugar content of a hothouse grape. Tomatoes are for the really professional grower. Someone suggested I grow Christmas trees. They would surely do well where the pines grow, as they do in our wood, but the Christmas tree and the pine are very different and to do really well good ground needs to be given over to a nursery scheme.

The truth is I was not cut out for any of these things as a commercial effort; it was the demand on my physical resources or, rather, a dislike of extremely hard work on the land that put me off. There was even more to it: I had been brought up with a certain disdain for what we called the 'wee croft' and the slavery of the individual working a plot. The hard life was, in a strangely contradictory way, regarded as the resort of dreamers with no discipline and little imagination! Bigotry happened to overlook the fact that the majority of crofts were well managed by hard-working people. The indolent crofter belongs in a remarkable far Cuillins dream that is quite unfair to him in his true situation. In my youth people engaged in 'respectable' farming would talk of smallholders 'scratching' away. These smallholders were to be found not only in England and Wales, where crofts are not found, but in Scotland too, where soldiers who had come back from the Great War were encouraged to settle on small acreages. In some places what had been respectable farms were purchased by the county authority and divided up into holdings. In others little holdings were laid out and rented to people who wanted to try their hand. The Smallholdings Act applying to holdings was framed in the late 1920s, and became law in 1928. In Scotland the tenancy of crofts goes back to an Act passed in the nineteenth century. Both deal with tenancies; under the Smallholdings Act there are different schemes whereby an occupier may rent and purchase over a long period, a sort of indefinite loan system. Beyond these schemes, there are wholly-owned holdings where people go it alone, supported by their pensions or some part-time job that makes life in a rural setting comfortable and economic to a certain degree.

The problem for many people seeking to live in this way is intensified by recent developments in communications. Everything has to be brought from towns, or from depots centred on large towns, and the smallholder must have transport. It costs money to shop and it costs money to get to market. It costs more for domestic fuel and life is made harder by all of these things as well as by the curtailment of local bus services and the closing down of railway branch lines. The sheep are undoubtedly going to be separated from the goats and those who can't take it will be forced to give up and go back within the barbican. Those who remain, and who go into the business, will look about in search of ways of diversifying the plan they originally opted for.

In the ordinary course of things a handbook for the small-holder is a very ambitious, not to say hopeful, venture, for in the patchwork of the smallholding world, directly regulated by a local authority, and on many other isolated little places which couples or small families work, what is needed is really an encyclopedia on how to make a pig ark, what breeds of pigs are best left to the well-equipped expert, how to incubate birds and thousands of other items of information large and small. No one man can tell the smallholder all he will want to know about land and animal husbandry in all its branches.

Those people already committed to working a holding have almost certainly carefully surveyed the possibilities of their undertaking. To take a holding without considering the market for produce or stock of different kinds would be reckless, but there are so many factors involved in going in. The ideal is a gentle southerly slope upon which the sun shines all day, but a Northumbrian slope to the sun will hardly grow vines! Keeping geese, attractive as they may be, won't make the smallholder rich, either at Michaelmas or Christmas, because there is no money in it any more: the goose has to be plucked, and plucking a goose is a terrible chore as well as a costly one if anyone has to be employed to do it. Not many people would do it for a pound!

All in all, the know-how of husbandry offered in the book that follows is intended to supplement what the smallholder already has, or to draw his attention to possible ways of diversifying what he already has in hand. There are whole books on many of the subjects dealt with, by experts in their field to whom the smallholder will sensibly turn for detail. Sometimes, however, there are things that have not been set down because they are not directly relevant to a particular study. A man may work practically single-handed putting up a post as big as a telegraph pole without a post auger. He may be stumped over the problem of straining a bit of fence wire without special tools or the kind of turnbuckle that makes the thing easy, or he may be unaware of the need to proceed with caution when he 'improves' the course of a ditch or dredges his pond to cleanse it. Land management, like its cultivation, is a specialized subject.

To get over difficulties the small man may toil in vain, thinking that he can't afford to hire a contractor to do what needs to be done. It is, of course, all a matter of capital and understanding what can be done by a once-off contract job. A guide is only of use to the man who can apply what is suggested. He pays his money and makes his choice, as he would, for instance, in poultry-keeping, where an electric incubator or an oil-fired one would be an extravagance and a broody hen hard to find. The individual is left to make up his mind, not just over the purchase of day-old chicks but also perhaps the economics of buying in point-of-lay pullets. The hard way is undoubtedly the heart-breaking way though it can prove the most satisfying, which is the ultimate end of any man's labour in any sphere, if what he is doing was worth doing in the first place.

Endorsing a book for the smallholder in his coat of many colours I find myself thinking how many of the things I shirked to tackle as a registered smallholder that I finally set out to do as a hobby. I kept sheep. I bred all kinds of birds – hens, bantams, pheasant and quail – and, although I doubt whether many smallholders go in for them, even white mice! I grew more vegetables and fruit than we could consume and gave them away, which may have made the life of some smallholder even harder in the end. I kept bees and still do so. I have faced the question of whether I would be indulging myself by the purchase of a chainsaw, a rotary cultivator, a rough grasscutter and many other items.

These are real problems for the man struggling to make his way on a small patch of ground. Even the farmer with capital makes a mistake and buys what proves to be a white elephant. This is largely what life is about, the exercise of uncommon sense when self-indulgence may be involved. My chainsaw proved a white elephant because it was a flexible drive off a cultivator. Its blade was inadequate for what I wanted, quite apart from the fact that such timber as I needed to fell was usually out of reach of the equipment and I had to resort to the old-fashioned feller's axe and the saw. A whole mountain of felled timber wouldn't have justified the purchase of that saw of course, and even the heavy rotary cultivator was wrong for my slope, and top-heavy. Not only that, but it chopped up convolvulus and the weeds multiplied ten-thousand-fold.

A guide to the smallholder undoubtedly runs the risk of insulting the intelligence of people who have come at it all the hard way, for they know from their own experience, but even they will be as eager as the author of this guide to save some other enthusiast from himself. We are not all made of the same stuff nor do we see the same snags. What is most important is that we should educate and continue to give the benefit of our experience to others.

I once designed and built an incubator and loaded it with quail eggs. On the day before I could expect the first movement within the shell there was a power cut which I didn't detect since I neither watched television, nor had occasion to cook at an electric stove or refer to an electric clock until the following day. The forty eggs were fatally chilled before I remembered about them. One quail hatched and died. I may not have achieved very much in husbandry but I had a lesson which I feel I might well pass on to anyone with the same kind of mind as my own.

The know-how offered hereafter is not all of this nature, but it is well sprinkled with timely warnings, which is as it should be. It is a crime to waste other people's time. It is sad to waste one's own and it is a duty to pass on the certain knowledge of what *not* to do.

IAN NIALL

FOREWORD

I would warn the person who lives in the city and cultivates a
dream of self-sufficiency that what the smallholder may *not*
do is charge double time for Sunday, or indulge himself by
observing the fourth commandment! Few smallholders have
a lot of time to spare when they keep stock or have land which
needs to be cultivated before the weather deteriorates. The
principal aim of this book is to provide guide-lines and to
pass on the experience gained in keeping stock, working in a
vinery and a greenhouse and cultivating land. There are
aspects of every branch of these subjects which will need to
be elaborated upon by those who are authorities on them.
Indeed I feel that it would be a mistake to attempt to be
specific about the varieties of fruit tree that might be grown
when one does well here and not at all well there, and
another is quite out of the question in a particular area.

Horticulture, the cultivation of arable land and its intensive cropping, as well as most aspects of animal husbandry,
are subjects to which specialists have devoted their whole attention. Advice of a specific nature is obtainable either
through bulletins and pamphlets from official sources – the
Ministry of Agriculture and Fisheries – or through depart-
ments of universities. There are many reference books available to the man who would be a specialist himself and learn
more about disease in the honey bee, blight on the plum or
sickness in the hen run. Guide-lines are what the words
mean, no more than common sense – a broad subject upon
which there is no single reference, no encyclopedia. People
with know-how would consider such a thing unnecessary.

This book is therefore not within a whole dictionary of the

last word, but rather the first one or two, offered in the hope that they may prevent a little of the heartache endemic in the business of running a smallholding or taking one on. A text book will provide information on how clay drains must be bedded and laid, how to make the perfect compost for mushroom growing and the way of coping with mildew in a vinery. This is a guide book and by no stretch of imagination can it be said to be the A, B, or C of smallholding, which is a very complex and many-sided business.

CJM

1

GOING INTO A LITTLE PLACE

It goes without saying that the commitment of a man who buys a holding is more serious than that of one who secures a tenancy. The reservations which the tenant may have will influence his landlord to a certain degree, whether the landlord happens to be the governing authority in that area or a private individual, and the agreement will have been vetted thoroughly to cover matters which either side considers imperative.

Outright purchase is a different matter. The beginner needs to have thought long and carefully before he decides to put down his money, for here he will perhaps be faced with a sink-or-swim situation and find it hard to recoup what he has laid out. The economics of such a transaction are such that where someone gives up, having failed to make a living, a would-be purchaser, who is soon aware of this fact, will hardly be offering the best price. Land may not depreciate in value but its value is not always based on the living it is likely to yield. Land as land is an asset, but a holding needs to be used as such, cultivated, operated as a unit and made to pay or provide a living. The decision to go in either as a tenant or as a freeholder may be made on the performance of some optimistic would-be seller or his agent with a glib tongue. Books may be made to show almost anything a clever book-keeper wants them to show, with minor assets written up and depreciation overlooked, or some kind of subsidy completely ignored because it happens to be convenient to do so. Where can the prospective purchaser look for advice? Solicitors will do all they can to uncover legal difficulties. An accountant can have the books to draft his own reading of a balance sheet and report on it.

All this may sound rather far out for a small venture but many people stare ruin in the face because of their reluctance to go into things thoroughly and objectively.

Beyond the consideration of whether the ground is suitable for the kind of scheme the beginner proposes to operate, or the possibility of changing things to improve chances, the asset to be acquired may seem ideal. A compact little holding on a hillside with a tree for shade and a few hens about the door might delight an artist looking for a suitable subject to sketch or paint, but the prospective tenant or purchaser must not be influenced by outward appearances. Access is important. Will the road stand its traffic or does it become water-logged and deteriorate into a series of mud channels in February when the dikes are full? Will the car or truck climb the hill in midwinter when there is snow and ice, and can its springs take the bumping and bouncing they will continually be subjected to on the rough bit half-way? Before the beginner is half-way there he has to think about how he will come out! The importance of the access road is high on his list of priorities.

Looking at the property itself (perhaps a rough sketch or a map has been provided) it seems reasonably compact. A cartographer might have shaded in the long tract of round rushes and the outcrops of rock on the contour lines, but the purchaser will walk the fields. What should he look for, supposing he has no real experience of such a transaction? If he can afford one he should look for a land surveyor, but supposing he cannot, he must look at gates and gateways, perimeter boundaries and what lies beyond them. Here, on the frontiers of his intended kingdom, he finds his everlasting problems of keeping things in or keeping things out, for this is what his work will depend upon. If he keeps stock, sheep perhaps, or pigs, he will discover that both have a tendency to seek the green grass on the other side of the hill. Without a barrier of wire mesh, pig-netting or sheep-netting, his herd or flock will be off. The first brush with a neighbour over a disaster like this may light the fires of a lasting feud.

The property is bounded by a stream perhaps, on the brink of which a beast stands ruminating; but the stream dries up in midsummer, or in winter its eroded banks are overbrimmed by the flood and most of the pasture is inundated. The novice needs second sight when he stands among the flags and the buttercups (which, incidentally, if he keeps a cow he can well do without). The holding may, of course, have been soundly fenced by a good landlord and well maintained by his tenant thereafter, but in some places soundly constructed boundaries have never existed and can be put up only at high cost. Here, old dry stone walls run into stone heaps and earth banks with a couple of thorn trees and a hank of sagging wire. The purchaser sees it all as sound enough until one day his wayward old ram bundles through the thorns, carries the loose wire on his back for a couple of yards and breaches the defences with the flock following on his heels into a fine patch of kale or a barley field. Where does he go from there? On and on, with his followers spreading out as they go! There will obviously have to be some improvement in the fence line, some renewal of wire between walls and hedgerow trees. The previous owner stopped the holes with thorns; this seems sound but thorns have a habit of crumbling and subsiding into the herbage and sheep have a way of seeing a hole that even the hazel triangle, rigged on the old ewe's neck like a collar, will pass through. Pigs, of course, can root and an old sow may be clever enough to lift a gate off its hinges, let alone move or bulldoze her way through a barrier that has no solid anchorage but looks good enough superficially.

Back at the stream and the ditches which are its minor tributaries, there may be more evidence of problems ahead. A neighbour pours his old oil into the ditch or pumps slurry out of his piggery and the ditch carries its polluted water through the cress bed. A flood builds a tidemark of contamination on land a mile away and where the plump Aylesbury paddled in the sun of the afternoon there is desolation and decaying vegetation to go with it. A good clean water supply and healthy ditches, even if they prove to be overgrown and silted, are what the do-it-yourself surveyor looks for.

He also looks at the lie of the land and places where in a dry spell there may be lush green grass for here are the boggy places which are likely to entrap his cultivator or his truck when he goes to and fro about the business of working his small acreage or feeding the stock he keeps. Land drains that have subsided and need renewing he marks on his notepad, not in the hope of having the vendor put them right, but to remind him of what he will one day need to do or positively have to do before his first year is out.

Where will he grow those early potatoes he hoped to grow to catch the market for local produce? Has the land been ploughed and what crops did well on it? The vendor may be vague about this but his neighbours will almost certainly have the history of the place. The landlord of the pub will say how often the vendor came in for a drink and how good a customer he was. Perhaps he drank his profit away? Perhaps he drank to drown his sorrows or perhaps he was just a lazy individual? A holding is what a man makes of it. A man is sometimes what his land makes him and there is as much danger in buying a place as in failing to make a go of it – an immediate loss of capital, and more poured down the drain, putting right things that should have been spotted in the first place. The lawyer employed will naturally have gone into the questions of restrictions of use, what may or may not be done on or with the land and even what stock may be kept, for instance, in some places, goats may be proscribed. There may be an injunction against the use of the place as a kennel or cattery, an objection to the setting up of a mink ranch which needs a licence, or some other intensive business of a special nature.

Beyond all this there is the simple wisdom of locals who

could advise against sowing or planting certain crops because of climate, soil condition, the prevalence of a particular pest or predator. Local knowledge in the matter of husbandry is even more important than a character reference concerning the previous owner or tenant. A spring crop may be devastated by the appearance of woodpigeons or collared doves or even by crows as the season for harvesting the spring sowing approaches. To have to fence with strong netting against foxes is enough to put a man off a scheme to have free-range birds. Pens for everything incline a man set on animal husbandry to look for a safer environment for his stock than one close to rough land in which predators and pests breed.

Having looked at the state of the land and its boundaries and water supply, there remains the nature of its protection from the wind – the kind of shade-trees that may grow in the open or along its hedges. A windbreak may be grown but a really satisfactory one takes some time to cultivate and the smallholder himself may be pressed for time. He looks to see the best and the worst of his bargain. Too many shade-trees deprive the land of nourishment for crops, too few make it a bleak place for wintering beasts. On a small acreage every square yard has to be nurtured and nursed to produce a crop of one sort or another, be it only grass across which those free-range birds may pick, or the tethered goat may browse. Land that is clear and clean of thistles, nettles and ragwort can often have more than its share of bracken or gorse. Nettles prove almost as hard to eradicate as bracken on certain types of soil but pigs are the answer to bracken, providing they can be confined to where the bracken is. One of the surest ways of breaking up and finally destroying bracken is to turn the field over to the rooting pigs. Bracken spreads because it has rhizomes. It doesn't depend on seeding and spreading as the seed is scattered. It isn't greatly discouraged by being ploughed once or twice but the pig's snout cultivates the ground, digs out the rhizome over and over again until the plant is exhausted and dies in the broken-up sods.

Gorse has to be fired, like heather, in the early part of the year and it will grow again, fortified by the potash the embers provide unless the man tackling it has the time to hack out the roots and burn these too. The gorse root is hard to unearth and where a mattock won't do a plough may serve. The alternative is to crop the new growth again and again until the root dies in the ground. Even so the dead root will be almost as big a nuisance to the cultivator as quitch or couch grass.

A clean patch is what the smallholder hopes to find, land with all the signs of diligent cultivation and careful husbandry, for he may otherwise simply be embarking upon an endless battle against the jungle with little time between skirmishes to make a living from the land he has won. The everyday nuisances may be compromised with and tolerated to a degree but there are some, like clearing scrub, overcoming the encroachment of blackthorn and bramble, that will be a burden to the strongest. It is, I am afraid, easier to buy trouble than to eradicate it once it has been purchased.

There are tasks quite beyond the power of a single man, tasks such as drainage improvement which need to be tackled with special equipment, draining ploughs (grants may be obtained for improvements of this kind) or the J.C.B. Here in the free enterprise department, which is the very stuff of the smallholder's way of life, a project must be well thought out and advice taken on the best way of doing it. The major excavating tool can perform unbelievable miracles in a matter of a few hours but the equipment and the skilled operator both come high. To get things right from the start generally proves cheapest in the long run. Landscaping of any kind avoiding the cost of mechanical equipment is something for the man who believes he will live for ever!

Whatever the previous use of the land may have been the new occupier will find things he would have otherwise – water supply to a market garden plot, water to outbuildings, a hard stand for a car or truck, a shed for the standing-out cattle or horses he may graze on his bit of pasture. These things may, according to the plan, be immediate changes or long-term projects. The pattern of cultivation is pretty well preset even under a rotation system for vegetables as it is in the standard farming of roots and corn. Most things have to be subjected to a change of ground; for instance, brassicas should never be grown twice on the same plot. The application of these simple laws of land care leave the smallholder with a programme he can vary if he has decided upon drastic change of use, such as the installation of greenhouses or the creation of deep litter or battery houses.

The outbuildings already on the property are of great importance, for their suitability will affect or even positively lay down what can or cannot be done in a scheme of husbandry. The state of outbuilding is almost equally important, for upkeep can be expensive and the jobbing builder employed, if there is money to engage his services, will want his cash before the smallholder earns it.

In general the nature of construction of the buildings purchased will govern maintenance. Old stone buildings may be structurally as sound as the rock upon which they have been set down, but they will usually be without a damp course such as a layer of slate to prevent the wet rising on the plastered wall within. Brick structures may be in need of pointing. Asbestos walls are only as good as the timber frame to which they have been attached. Corrugated iron or 'tin' sheds that are heavily coated with bitumastic paint may be suspect when the corrugated iron has been overlaid here and there to cover perforation which even bitumen cannot conceal. This applies on the roof as well as the walls. The only way to be sure of the soundness of the roof is to see the under-

25

side within the whole area covered. Supporting posts and beams and rafters with a strong smell of creosote or Cuprinol have been recently treated for woodworm. A knock with a hammer will make the residue of beetle borings emerge from the holes as a fine powder. The point of a knife can indicate unsound beams and timbers. Posts that have been clad with galvanized iron may be shaky and this kind of thing, while it seems a carping point, may, if ignored, lead to a whole structure having to be brought down and rebuilt. A stable with a hanging door, a shed with a roof that rises in the gale, a draughty shippon, a piggery into which water from the adjoining roof constantly seeps, all spell trouble – and hardship for the stock they are expected to house. The old hen-house is no bargain if it is taken 'as is' in its dilapidated condition with a layer of droppings ten years old and nest boxes full of rat's nest litter. A property in this condition has to be cleared out, cleaned thoroughly and disinfected so that neither parasites nor infection of any kind remain. Again, this spells labour in addition to the everyday business of making a living, and for even the most hard-working individual there are only a set number of hours in the day.

The ideal steading or group of buildings, like the ideal land for cultivation, is hard to come by, if it exists anywhere. No one vacates the ideal holding and everyone going in compromises on the matter of buildings and their condition. A nail-sick roof cries out for the whole thing to be lifted off and new timbering done, but here there is expense and in the absence of a man skilled in the slater's craft it may be expedient to skim the roof with cement, binding the slates to one another and adding a little weight to the roof at the same time. In this case the rafters must be sound for these take the weight. Occasionally corrugated iron may be fixed to replace the old slates but it is a question of whether the tin roof will last longer than the skimmed slate roof.

If there are no major defects in the structure of the outbuildings, the prospective smallholder, should consider in his bargaining how the buildings are served by water and lighting and how they will do if he wants to use them for brooders and an incubator, supposing he is going in for the raising and selling of chicks, or as a hygienic dairy where walls and floor must be more than sound and able to be kept spotlessly clean. Milk and cheese are products that come under the eye of the Public Health Department who will call to inspect and approve the dairy and the milking parlour or shed when produce is to be sold to the public. A dairy needs to have a piped water supply, facilities for scalding vessels, and equipment such as strainers, separators and so on. The sterilization of everything connected with milk production is vital.

Once again, the incomer will have a certain inheritance from the man who sold him the property, perhaps in the approval of the set-up by the authority concerned or, on the other hand, a serious objection to the state of things being allowed to continue! Without asking questions and assuring himself that everything is as it should be, the incomer may find that what he has bought is condemned and almost everything needs to be renewed. There are points of law in all this of course, but it can be that the vendor has debts which forced him to sell and the money paid over is already in someone else's pocket before the true nature of things is discovered. The life of many smallholders is beset with problems of hire purchase, mortgage and loans. The purchaser needs more to go on than a word or a seemingly honest face.

On the domestic side, where the living quarters are of the same vintage as the rest of the property, there are additional things to be looked at – water pipes, wiring, the efficiency of water-heating, the cooking stove. There is no problem in installing a gas stove with cylinders situated outside the house, though gas under these circumstances may be as expensive as electricity, but a great many country dwellings are served by stoves of the Esse and Aga type that burn solid fuel. In these the thing to look at is the condition of the boiler and the ovens. Many old stoves are conversions from solid fuel to oil and are not as efficient as those designed for the purpose. Both, to remain efficient, need to be overhauled and looked at annually. Oil-burners require attention more frequently to avoid trouble. The solid-fuel stove can be persuaded to work with an unsuitable fuel but the oil-burner cannot.

Having looked at all these things and decided that he has a reasonable deal, the would-be smallholder is ready to embark upon an operation that will surely absorb all his time and all his thought, seven days a week, from the day he goes into his little place.

2

TOOLS FOR THE JOB

Tools are the mainstay of life on the land whatever the nature of the work being done. Without good equipment and accessories labour is often twice as expensive in both time and money. What tools to buy and what to avoid? Some implements suffer from what the accountant marks down under depreciation and their value second-hand may not justify a bid when they are put up as individual items. Others are basic to almost any kind of husbandry and are none the worse for being old. Their age may often indicate their soundness and reliability.

Tools that are powered have a habit of showing their defects, not when they are turned over to demonstrate that they start or run, but when they have been under heavy use for a while. An engineer or mechanic knows, of course, the signs which may indicate trouble to come. The efficiency of an engine lies in its bearings, piston and cylinder. Its seeming soundness may be due to the fact that a heavier oil has been put in as a temporary expedient while it is being put up for sale. There may even be sawdust in the gearbox to make it appear that the gears mesh without complaint!

The tools that are sold in job lots are hand implements. Individual items are a different matter. In the hand tools an old pinchbar or crowbar lies among a selection of forks, picks, mattocks. The well-forged pick or mattock is little the worse for having a worm-eaten handle for it can easily be fitted with a new shaft. The rake can be given dental treatment. Spades are a little less of a bargain when they have had wear but most people know the quality of the hand tool they would use and how much they might wisely spend on things that will be of general use.

The larger tools are an investment hardly to be avoided but the smallholder looking at the morning sky through rose-tinted spectacles may see himself with a thing like a 70cm

(28in) chainsaw. Every item he buys that doesn't really earn his living is capital tied up and often capital wasted. A chainsaw, for instance, can be an absolute godsend when the old tree has to be taken down, for wood makes good fuel, but would it be wise to invest in a saw, and which of the many saws available should one choose? Logs can be made with a small saw. A tree can be brought down with an axe and a crosscut; it can even be cut up with the crosscut although this is a long and painful operation. The man who buys the heavy duty, 70cm (28in) either has money to spare or intends to make his place the centre of a logging business. Even a large saw can be rented by the day from a contractor though it could turn out that the man renting it might as well have let his tree lie and bought his logs from somewhere else.

To return to the question of powered tools and mechanized items of equipment, since the spade will never do, when it comes to land cultivation what the professional market gardener would use represents about the minimum. The machine really needs to be solid and sound with a power unit of nothing less than 5hp capable of taking a solid toolbar and, when needed, towing a dumper or mini-wagon. The outlay will be around £1000 for the machine with cultivating and pick tines, weeding discs and so on. Where the machine is used in row cultivation, making furrows and setting them up after planting, it may have to take a fair-sized ploughing attachment and then the investment will be in a small tractor of about 35hp perhaps, one capable of towing gang cultivators controlled by the operator from the driving seat, where, on a more modest scale, the machine involved might have been one of those walk-behind cultivators with off-set handles.

There is no way of laying down a hard and fast rule about selection of equipment for cultivation; much depends on the land. In a heavy clay soil it goes without saying that the equipment needs to be particularly robust and heavier than that used on a sandy, light soil. On a slope there are other considerations. Even the method of cultivation may be in question when there is danger of soil being worked downhill. In some cases a cultivator with rotary tines plays havoc by cutting up convolvulus, mare's tail and couch grass. The self-propelled machine eats its way along a slope in a satisfactory manner so long as there are no rocks, but slopes are often best managed up- and downhill to avoid erosion.

Before new equipment is purchased it pays to have a particular machine demonstrated on the ground it is required to cultivate. The supplier of this kind of equipment will be only too pleased to demonstrate and, since he hopes to sell more than one machine, will advise on the right tool for the job. However, there are so many machines of like design that the smallholder needs to look around and see what may have served someone else in the same line of husbandry. There are many considerations and the most important of them is the robust construction of the machine itself. Are the castings heavy enough? Will it vibrate to the point of fatigue and crack and fall apart? Some items may easily be replaced but a base casting fracturing may make the machine little more than junk. The light machine may do the job but will it last and is the heavy machine something with powered axle or a piece of equipment that in the ordinary way moves forward on the bite of its tines? How many forward and reverse speeds does it have and is the gearbox one that tends to give a lot of trouble? Every piece of farm machinery in regular seasonal use suffers from extreme wear and tear and begins to go downhill in the end. Cultivating a few rows of cabbages and carrots may be done well enough with a walk-behind machine capable of cultivating to a depth of 30cm (1ft) (not everyone will find his loam fertile at this depth!) and a width of just over 1m (3ft 6in). It depends on the nature of the land once again, but the more robust machine is the heavier one. When it is taxed with a particularly difficult terrain to turn over there is a considerable variation possible in the set-up of slashers which cut the turf and bury the surface growth of weeds, finger tines which produce the final tilth or picks which may be needed to break hardened clay or dig a trench for the cultivation of some special crop. The 'furrower' used on the toolbar can only be effective on the heavier type of machine. On a light cultivator used on the domestic garden it is not the most useful of items but on the right machine the furrower, weeders, hoeing blades and cultivating feet can reduce the number of passes necessary to keep a plot in the right condition.

A great deal of thought has gone into the design and manufacture of these small-scale machines. While many of the larger machines used on farms have inspired scaling-down, the dividing line between garden, market garden and small farm equipment begins to be obscured. The grass-cutter is a case in point where the revolving cutter may be towed by a full-sized tractor to mow large areas of ground. The Allen scythe, on the other hand, was undoubtedly an adaptation of the cutterbar principle of the conventional hay-reaper. In this sphere of operation there are again innumerable variations in methods of keeping down grass and 'wild' undergrowth and there is a great variety of machines from which to choose.

In some places, where the undergrowth is supported by hard-fibred plants and thorns the machine needs to cut with a much greater ground clearance than is required on a lawn. Once again the engine takes the brunt, and its name and reliability are important, as is the method of starting. Many a man spends almost as long getting going as he does actually performing the task with a machine under-powered and prone to overheating or oiling up. Here too, the lie of the land may impose a burden of a particular kind, when cutting in one direction drains a bearing on one side. This often causes oil to burn off in exhaust fume – resulting in overheating and unreasonable wear, alternating on the return journey when the angle of operation is reversed. A heavy-duty machine costs more but being what it is, will perform better in the long run, whereas a lighter item may have to be retired to the toolshed to become a white elephant.

The second-hand value of the unwanted item is never very great. Most people regard a second-hand machine as one that has been overworked on some task for which it proved inadequate. The rough grasscutter is no exception. It really needs to be able to take the rough and shear through brush and bramble as well as bracken and fern while clearing the occasional stone. The best machine trundles on like a tank even when the foliage it is chopping up is wet; though anyone who puts even the most sound equipment under such strain as cutting thick grass in a very wet condition needs to have money to burn: certainly he has no feeling for an engine and its reasonable workload.

Manufacturers are, of course, aware of the stresses and strains put upon their product and do their best to safeguard their name by designing accordingly. Some machines have a great reputation for slogging on and performing into their old age like the finest vintage car. These always have the most sound design principles and the most reliable components and in fact stand in contradiction of the claim that manufacturers deliberately design with 'built-in destruct'.

It is perhaps less difficult to recommend machines for cultivation on the flat than to take into account the methods of cultivation on slopes and machines best suited to this purpose. A great many machines will perform almost as well on the slope as they do on the flat but on flat ground there is always the nature of the land itself to consider. In an area such as parts of the Fen country where the depth of fertile soil is measured in metres rather than centimetres and there is no claybed or hard pan or the slightest undulation of infertile subsoil, the average market garden walk-behind cultivator can be substituted for a machine that transports its operator. In either case the workload will be constant or almost constant the variation being one resulting from the extremes of heavy rainfall and frost. When the land is badly waterlogged it is practically impossible to work and in severe frost it can't be turned because it is too hard.

An initial investment in an easy starting, robust machine with a variety of tools is undoubtedly the best bet. The operator who rides will last longer even though some of the machine's power output is absorbed in carrying him along. This outlook may apply in other branches of husbandry of course, and a great many people plump for going along for the ride as is borne out by the increasing popularity of mini-tractors for grass-cutting, cultivating and the movement of crops and compost materials. However, once again, the smallholder may be indulging himself in the same way as he was tempted to do when he thought of the chainsaw. Running costs have to be taken into account. The drive and the gearbox are under strain enough perhaps when the machine runs hour after hour preparing the plot, producing a sowing tilth, or making ridges for planting. The one-man operation may need to take into account not so much the wear and tear on the human body or simply the wear and tear on the mechanical horse, as the bank balance and the possible need for renewed credit.

Given that money can be raised for the outlay, and account taken of depreciation, there are a number of names in the business that are already household words by virtue either of the reliability of the product or, it must be said, the intensity of advertising campaigns! People who are inclined to make a dilettante approach fall for gimmicks and have fantasies in which they see themselves bustling about on scaled-down Fergusons making their sometime faithful Adam seem like Methuselah. The smallholder in the business to make a living will be steered clear of the 'domestic wonder' by most reputable implement suppliers. They know that he will soon be back reproaching them for sales pressure and asking for a deal on some more useful item than a miniature cart in which the great dane had a ride through yews and cypress trees. The crucial questions are what tool and what make.

Not everyone, purchaser or maker, will automatically approve of the makes and types dealt with hereafter. It must be emphasized that there are other makes and those dealt with are recommended simply because the author has had experience with them, seen them in use over a considerable period of time, and has no information to suggest that they are anything but entirely reliable. Without doubt someone, somewhere will have had trouble with one or another of them, a particular model which did not do well on a piece of ground where there were problems. I have faced difficulties on sloping ground where the soil is light using machines of different makes and with accessories that might have been fine on the flat but were no good on a steep incline. The same may apply to adaptations for cutting grass. On rough ground the machine cannot be anything but self-propelled and needs good traction. The heavy-duty machine costs a lot more but is the best investment in the long run.

In cultivators there is little to choose between those with names like Merrytiller, made by Wolesley Webb, the Estate and Monarch made by Mountfield, the Landmasters and the celebrated Howards. Where the weight of the engine is situated, the kind of drive, the choice of speeds, the clutch and gearbox are considerations and here the user cultivates personal preferences. What he may tolerate in a grasscutter – a two-stroke engine – he may curse on a cultivator and the horsepower rating of the machine governs what it will do and how long it will live to do it on heavy land. Powered wheels, whether by chain drive or a system of V-belts – the Merrytiller and others of similar design are chain-driven, the

Mountfield Estate and Monarch are V-belt machines – take the backache out of the job.

The smaller machines which 'eat' their way along, pulled by the operation of slashers or pick blades, require some holding, especially when they veer downhill. Landmasters, Mountfields and Merrytillers all take grass-cutting attachments and have a variety of set-ups employing extensions. Most of these machines will do all that is ever asked of them, but on virgin ground are really best employed on a narrow strip using the minimum number of slashers or cultivating tines in the first instance. Once the land is well broken the facility of broader strip cultivation immediately recommends itself.

The weight of the engine is generally balanced over the drive shaft, but the Mountfields mentioned shun this principle and make a point of counterbalance which may suggest a more positive control where the light soil on a slope may be in danger of being worked downhill. It isn't always practical to cultivate up- and downhill and this doesn't in any case guarantee that the topsoil won't end up at the bottom of the hill after a few seasons. Howard's Gem is really outside the realm of the part-time gardener, it is more for the professional with a considerable acreage to turn over. Being a heavier machine with three forward gears and one reverse, and weighing between 270 and 360kg (600 and 800lb), it doesn't carry its operator, who walks behind, but it does a man-sized job with a 10hp engine (four-stroke petrol or diesel). There are, of course, lesser Howards, the 350 which is a V-belt model with four forward speeds. Howard equipment goes on up into the arable farming business with a selection of rotovators for use on tractors with power take-off.

Unlike the car business, second-hand equipment – machines that have worked well and look well – is hard to come by. This is because in most cases where they do the job they were bought to do, the machines work on until they are no longer worth reconditioning. The model and the year are not as important as the acreage they plough! A machine that gives trouble will be disposed of, but no one wants it. The man who goes in for the well-known and well-tried machine can rely on the name. Spares are only a problem when he happens to break down in the middle of the cultivating or harvesting season. A lesser drawback is that between whiles everyone has their servicing done and the depot tends to have work piled up to the doors.

Rough grass-cutting or modest hay-making using a machine with a cutter-bar and the hay reaper's reciprocating action, are no problem when the machine is robust enough for the job and it must, of course, be self-propelled. Such a stipulation tends to put the oiling-up, moody two-stroke out of consideration altogether. A reliable engine like the Briggs and Stratton practically ensures immediate response. Here again, however, thought must be given to the angle at which such engines are required to operate. No engineer would be entirely happy with the theory that the return cut lets bearings on the opposite side become immersed in oil, for no matter what, this can mean that bearings are deprived of lubricant for half their operating time.

It is amazing how the heavy-duty machine accepts punishment on occasion. The Allen series of machines hardly needs recommendation. They are among the most popular on the market. The Challenger Commercial has a Briggs and Stratton four-stroke with belt drive to a cutter disc with four reversible cutting blades. The slightly smaller engine of the JLO Challenger is a two-stroke, though it powers a machine doing an identical job. Hayters take a larger bite at things with a ratchet-drive machine called the Condor powered by an 8hp four-stroke. There are many other machines for the rough grass of course, and innumerable versions of the lawn-mower from the one with the diminutive two-stroke to the cricket pitch mower which runs on a tractor's take-off unit.

Tools for the job are to be recommended when they are used for the purpose for which they were originally designed. Rarely does the accessory surpass the main feature. A cultivator is a cultivator first. It may serve as a grader, bulldozer, yard-scraper, wagon, weeder, or have a power take-off of sorts enabling it to operate a saw of some kind. It will hardly ever perform these tasks as well as a tool specifically designed for the job. The man who needs to move a lot of stuff needs a powered truck. The man who really needs a cultivator shouldn't wear out the engine making it cut rough grass with perhaps a variation in its transmission system that it wasn't intended to take.

There are many kinds of tools that are special to a purpose, like boring post holes, which can be made with a hand-operated borer or auger, or a power-tool. Such things can be

rented by the day or the week along with concreting equipment, heavy drills, electric hammers, percussion drills, flame guns, sprays and a whole range of building equipment including generators and pumps. Use for these tools on a smallholding may well occur infrequently and need will never justify their purchase so that it is as well to find out what is available in your particular district. Being a borrower can be costly, and embarrassing when something breaks or burns out and there is no insurance cover. No one ever has all the tools he needs for all the jobs he would do, and rental, although it may be costly, gets over the problem when a job can't be put off and know-how restricts the method of going about it.

There are, of course, many ways of getting by; most of them are expensive in time, and time is what the average smallholder learns to use sparingly. There are never enough hours in his day.

3

MANAGEMENT –
WAYS AND MEANS

The management of a holding, whether it is used as arable land, operated as an animal husbandry project of one sort or another, or devoted to something like cultivation under glass, involves the use of water. There are many ways in which an occupier may find himself in confrontation with his neighbour and, if boundaries and fences stand highest on the list, water always comes a close second. The ways in which the rights of others may be infringed are not always obvious. Main water supply apart – and few farmers or smallholders would care to rely entirely upon piped water – the water problem arises not only from the weather in a particular season but also from other things such as the state of the land drains or the cleanliness of the ditches.

The most enthusiastic smallholder can make mistakes when tackling ditches and often the trouble is caused by the land drains being disturbed or crushed. The map, where there is one, may show old marsh dotted with the symbol of round rushes and reeds. Marshland can only be tackled by massive machinery in a large-scale project involving surveyors and civil engineers. But that patch of boggy ground is something else: it was under cultivation once and now machinery gets bogged down. What happened to ruin the prospect of cultivating the ground and raising a crop?

This is a chicken and egg question when it comes down to it, for the neglect of a ditch can slow the drainage of land. Where drain tiles are buried they silt up because the outflow diminishes. The weather takes a hand and the tiles are dislocated in a severe frost or moved by the machinery that is driven over them. Excavation might reveal the trouble or it might simply release backed-up water to make a slough of even more fertile ground. The whole thing becomes complicated when a survey reveals that it would be unwise to widen or deepen the ditch, since this kind of remedy serves only where the watercourse continues to be adequate beyond the boundary.

There is another problem in the maintenance of drains and the management of water supply. To make any sort of improvement it is almost always essential to slow the inflow and tackle the problem from top to bottom. A temporary dam will increase the level on one side of the property and decrease it on the other. Unless the work is undertaken after consultation with neighbours and in a dry part of the season – never in February! – one neighbour may complain that his ditch overflows and ruins his crop and the other shriek that his cattle are without water unless he carries it to them. Allowing for a satisfactory agreement on either side, the cleaning of the low-level ditch can go ahead but here care must be taken not to deepen holes or widen banks or the water-logged area may increase before a new land drain can be laid or damaged tiles can be located and replaced.

There are many other aspects of the business that make it one for consultation not only with neighbours but with officials – the River Board – who will advise and have a lot to say about the extraction of water from the stream! There may be a rate to be paid if water is channelled and not returned clear and clean as it was in the first place. Even a flour mill has had to battle over water channelled to the mill wheel by a millrace cut and returned to the stream thirty yards farther on. Water pumped to cisterns located in fields may deprive other people downstream of their lawful supply and if everyone did the same the supply of water might dry up completely.

There are ways of catching water that are outside the control of the local authority altogether. It is not illegal to collect water from the roofs of buildings and use it for any purpose though it may have to be treated for harmful bacteria, midges and mosquito larvae. In some places where water is particularly precious cisterns are set up with sloping concrete 'wings' which serve the same purpose as the roof drainage. There is nothing to stop this kind of supply being piped or pumped to any part of a holding short of water and the supply used to irrigate cultivation strips where this can be contrived with polythene pipe. However, there are minor drawbacks. Polythene is attractive to all kinds of burrowing animals, voles and mice, for instance. It is also easily picked up when it is buried. Pick tines on a cultivator will damage it unless the pipeline is well defined or runs on a headland.

These difficulties overcome, water may easily be supplied to a number of drinking places equipped with the old-fashioned enamel bath with a ball-cock rigged to control the level or to top up the old porcelain sink used as a trough. Drinking water must be purified and filtered but irrigation water need not be treated. Nevertheless, it is wise to cover the main cisterns with heavy black polythene or a substantial lid to prevent algae growing and a chain of bacteria developing.

Water for domestic consumption must come from a well or spring approved by the health authority, even where the well has been used for generations without ill-effect. The infestation of a well by harmful bodies of one sort or another is not rare. What usually happens is that the old user acquires a degree of immunity which the new smallholder will not have. Another set-back to owning a well is that the smallholder may be levied on his assessment as the possessor of a well of drinkable water. He may then wonder if he should not have taken up the matter of a piped water supply the moment he discovered that the property was without one.

Given an adequate set of fences, walls and hedges and a reliable source of water, the incomer needs to maintain all in good order. But he has many other things that require maintenance — walls and roofs, as well as floors. His electricity supply may come on poles from the transformer unit and the meter-box on the boundary, and may be entirely his responsibility. Along this line he may once or twice be faced with the problem of erecting something as big and heavy as a telegraph pole. The post auger is the perfect tool for making a hole and a powered one is ideal. Even so there is some know-how involved in elevating the pole and setting it in place and the man lacking the money to hire labour and equipment must consider other ways and means of doing this kind of thing.

The stepped-trench method of putting up a wooden pole is very old and can hardly be improved upon where resources are limited. The pole's intended position is carefully marked on the ground. Let us say that the pole is 9m (30ft) long and required to stand 8m (26ft) above ground level. The hole needs to be just over 1.2m (4ft) deep and a little wider than the diameter of the pole. A trench is dug with a series of steps along it, each 30cm (1ft) in length, the width of the pole, and 23 to 25cm (9 to 10in) deep. These lead to a further section dug even deeper making a step down of

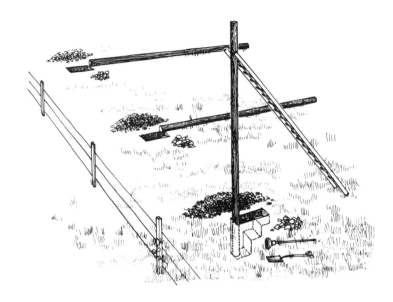

another 30 to 45cm (12 to 18in) leading to yet another, shorter, step of roughly the same depth. The pole is rolled into the trench and slid until its base is a few centimetres from the end. This will enable the top end of the pole to be elevated until the length inclines at an angle allowing a ladder to be introduced between the incline and the ground. The ladder is then thrust against the pole until the pole is forced upright to drop into the hole it is intended to occupy. This done, it is a simple matter of filling in and consolidating the trench. If necessary the pole can be braced in position until the hole has been enlarged round it for the pouring of concrete with reinforcing rods. (Needless to say the pole must be a seasoned one and treated with preservative whether it is to be cemented in or not.)

Putting up a rough shed or a cattle shelter can be dealt with in the same way and the first pole used, once it is firmly fixed, for the elevation of those at the other corners of the structure. A block and tackle is all that is needed to do this and investment in a locking tackle is well worth while when it comes to tree-felling, a business which calls for some expertise unless the whole process of felling is controlled by ropes and slings. In this case the amateur may avoid the snag of getting either his axe or his saw trapped since straining the tree keeps the sawcut open and enables one to lower the tree into the right area. A careless approach may damage slate roofs or tiles.

Almost as important to the man who does his own repair work is a crawler ladder which hangs over the ridge and allows the amateur slater or tiler to work his way down replacing broken sections with new material. A similar device is easily made for a greenhouse that has to be tackled in this way. By using the ridge, polythene can be easily fixed on the glazing bars by means of slats. The slats are treated with creosote before they are nailed in place. Polythene repairs are effective for a couple of seasons at least, although it must be remembered that this is a material that tends to harden in the sunlight. After two years it will generally fragment and take off in the wind.

On the subject of walls and their maintenance it must be said that few amateur bricklayers are competent enough to undertake the rebuilding of a main structure where walls have bulged and the roof needs to be supported while the work goes on. But many a man who gets a 'brickie' to put in footings – the foundation and first course – can make a fair stab at building a wall. The principal requirements are a little surveying, the use of the level and the plumb bob and line, a trowel and a bolster and an improvised hod where there is need for any scaffolding. If the bricks are seconds they must be carefully cleaned and soaked. The mixing of mortar to the precise plastic state a professional would insist upon is beyond most amateurs but there is ready-mix and the only things to be careful about here are to avoid making the mix too wet or trying to make too much at a time. 'Hasten slowly' is the best maxim. Forget how many bricks a professional bricklayer can lay in a day: building fast may result in the whole thing having to be knocked down and redone. In any kind of walling the job must be undertaken with care. Even clearing a rubble-cored wall that needs restoring should be approached with caution for it must be remembered that the outer parts of the wall are only a shell and an avalanche of rubble can result from over-enthusiastic tidying up.

Most stone walls take time to build because of the irregular shape of the stone from which they are constructed. When a limestone rubble wall breaks at the coping stones it must be brought down to a point where the outer shell remains sound. The rebuilding must be tackled from this level with the utmost care to see that the outer parts are mortared and set before the rubble filling goes in, or the whole thing may buckle and spill down once again. When the rebuilding is complete the coping stones have to be firmly mortared and the top made watertight for if the top is not well done rain will get in, water will freeze and break the bonding mortar. The same sort of thing will happen should elderberry or ivy take root in cavities. The tools for walling of this kind are the trowel and the maul or the heavy hammer. Building is the better for the close fitting of stone rather than lavish mortaring.

Rebuilding minor damage to a dry-stone wall calls for a good eye. A dry-stone wall is well keyed and the selection of stone is half the art of the business now largely the work of a few skilled craftsmen in their own particular locality.

Fencing is a different matter; here the amateur may go out and buy fenceposts. If he is particularly lucky and has oak logs of a suitable length he may split the logs into posts or get them split and never need to replace any of them again. He may use elm when disease makes the felling of elms necessary. Elm has great resistance to water and makes a good, tough post. Straining the wire, like making the post holes, may be done with a special set of fencing equipment, but holes may also be made with a crowbar and there is a way of straining wire that old soldiers who fought in the First World War were taught. The ordinary wire is looped to a yard or two of barbed wire. The fence strand is fixed to the first post in the usual way and strained very simply into position on posts farther along by wrapping the barbed wire round a levering post. As the lever is used the barbs bite into this post and then tighten the wire running through the staples of the whole length. These staples are then hammered home and the barbed wire is used to draw the next strand of fence wire tight for the stapling to be done and the staples driven in. The job takes two men, and serves well where short stretches of fence are needed.

The encroachment of bracken and its final eradication by the use of pigs has already been mentioned, but there are, of course, other scourges. Gorse, for instance, that can in due season be treated with fire, although this never really gets to the root of the trouble unless the treatment is followed up with the use of a mattock or some kind of grubber to get the roots out. Indeed, if this is not done, a second growth of gorse will result and this will be stronger and darker in colour by virtue of the potash supplied by burning the first. In the case of convolvulus or an infestation of coltsfoot, never rely on the rotary cultivator, for this only encourages the plant to spread. Nuisances like this and mare's-tail must be got out of the turned furrow and where possible, removed from the subsoil at the same time. Few pernicious weeds can be exhausted. Couch grass needs to be harrowed out and burned along with convolvulus, mare's-tail and coltsfoot. Leaving any of these to rot is a forlorn hope and in fact ensures that they remain on the ground to take over again when they have been hidden by other vegetation or rolled in

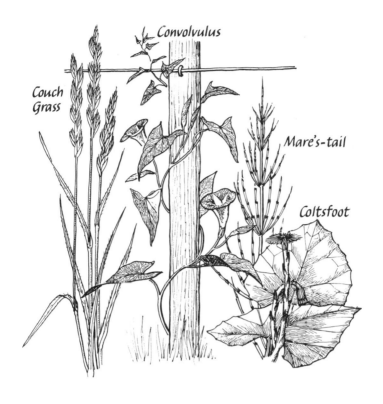

Couch Grass

Convolvulus

Mare's-tail

Coltsfoot

by implements used on the headland. Backache is what the eradication of perennial weeds is about. Few of the bigger nuisances really succumb to the widely-advertised remedies which in use barely affect the surface growth and discourage the root structure hardly at all, though they are listed as good for almost every known tough-rooted weed as well as brush-wood.

There are, of course, a great many sprays which may be used with effect on the common weeds of the field and hedge-row. Most of them are described as 'selective' in their effect. The gamble lies in whether, on the final balance sheet, there is any advantage in drastically reducing certain weeds:

it could involve the elimination of seed-eating birds, the destruction of useful flies and insects – useful in that they pollinate plants and are predatory on certain harmful insects – and even the loss of a growth useful in a nitrogen cycle essential to all plant life. It is up to the individual to decide whether or not to use spray insecticide. Undoubtedly the manufacturer will present a wonderful argument on crop yield but how much of the final result derives from the use of the spray is debatable. A great many people are now as much against sprays as they are against the use of artificial manures and the over-stimulation of the soil.

A word must be said about a different kind of spraying to preserve the crop on the furrow, of course, for here it cannot be denied that it is a foolish man who hopes to save money and earn his reward by leaving things to nature. In this department advice on specific sprays such as those for blight can be obtained from the Ministry of Agriculture.

A department of land management that always requires attention is that involving animal pests such as woodpigeons, collared doves, rabbits, rats and mice as well as birds like the house sparrow. On small patches of ground it is possible to net a cultivated plot with something like Netlon, which is made of nylon and doesn't rot although it has a frustrating way of hitching itself to almost every stick and stalk it is stretched over and really needs to be supported by a frame.

On larger areas woodpigeons and collared doves, which in some places have become the greater menace, can be discouraged with bright foil bird-scarers and the old-fashioned scarecrow who is hardly worth his money most of the time, familiarity breeding contempt. Detonating bird scarers have a monotony about them that manufacturers have never thought to break. It is likely that the determined flock of pigeons becomes accustomed to the regularity of the detonations. There is another method being tried at the moment, involving the doping of the birds which can then be picked up and destroyed, but this has a degree of barbarity about it that repels anyone concerned to see that animals are not made to suffer in the process of keeping them from eating a crop.

The catch-up kind of trap will not work well with the crow because it is not movable. Crows are too mobile on potato rows where the earthing up has not been done very well. This can be remedied, but it takes a shot to discourage crows once they arrive on the scene. Pigeons too, respond best to a hail of lead. If tackled from a hide for two or three days running they will generally give the place a clear berth for as many days afterwards. The house sparrow can only be tackled at the source – evicted from its home in the eaves of outbuildings. It is not illegal to destroy birds when they are actually attacking a crop. Even a pheasant can be shot out of season in these circumstances, but it is best, wherever possible, to net the crop against blackbirds who will, come what may, take a toll of the soft fruit ripening on the tree.

Ground pests are another matter. Here again there are diverging viewpoints on ways and means. Rats can be taken in the catch-alive kind of trap or eradicated by the use of a poison. The catch-alive trap needs to be inspected at regular intervals. Poisons are not all entirely selective and must be kept out of the way of domestic animals that might be made sick, if not killed, by them.

Care in the handling and distribution of foodstuff put in troughs for stock, so that there is no more in the trough than the stock will consume, will help to keep the rat population from gravitating to a property. There is also a need to keep stores of food, mash and pellets, in strong metal bins and in some cases to reinforce the lower parts of old doors with galvanized iron. Rats and mice follow scent and most animal foods attract the largely omnivorous rodent. It pays to be scrupulously careful with foodstuff and to sweep up and remove any residue that may attract the rat or mouse making his foray after dark. One or two cats will discourage rats and mice but only within a small area. Rats travel and tend to move to places where the pickings are better; the destruction they can achieve is quite horrifying and no one can afford them, even the most soft-hearted sentimentalist. There are county pest officers who will advise on how to deal with infestations and tackle the problem for the person suffering from the plague. However, prevention is better than cure and a little care over feeding stuff and how it is put down is the wisest precaution.

4

CROPS FOR MARKET

Before suggesting crops for market it is perhaps necessary to point out that there will generally be little hope of concentrating on a single kind of vegetable, or even on two or three. It would be unwise of anyone, whether he is sure of his market or not, to trust in the season. Although there are experts in every commercial sphere of husbandry all of them invest a fair amount of capital to overcome the worst of setbacks and enable them to continue on a specialist basis. To go into one of these fields without experience would be foolhardy in the extreme. However, one has a fair chance of success if one aims to cultivate a variety of produce, chosen by looking at such matters as supply and demand and at what others have been able to do in similar circumstances.

To begin with the humble potato, which usually provides a profitable crop and is reasonably economic in terms of labour, and which is perfectly happy to be grown alongside other vegetables. Nevertheless, it must be understood that there is a great deal of difference between 'growing a few spuds' and growing commercially. The essentials are: suitable ground with a furrow depth of between 18 and 25cm (7 and 10in), a reliable supply of good farm manure, a reasonable rainfall *and* a means of irrigating the acreage at the critical stage of growth.

The first decision will surely be whether to go for earlies and catch the market locally at the right time. Potatoes, as everyone knows, come flying in from foreign parts and there is no way someone in a locality where there is late frost and a cold wind can ever compete with the grower situated in a mild, seaboard area of the south. The early potato is a mid-summer product, maturing in the lengthening days. The maincrop, which has a much higher yield, is a post-summer potato and begins to reach its best as the summer ends. A maincrop then, is likely to be the choice, for second earlies are a compromise that hardly pay off.

What maincrop seed should the beginner buy? There are a number of considerations, quite apart from the suitability of a chosen variety for the land in which it is to be planted, and among these is the sort of potato that the housewife turns out of the pot. The housewife who really knows her potatoes and doesn't buy them prepacked likes one that looks like a potato, even when she overboils it. She expects a roasted potato to look like a roasted potato. The grower who sells round the doors or to the gourmet's hotel should know his customer's preference. A lot of people who know the mashed potato on the plate would be surprised to learn how many varieties of potato there are. Some are scant of foliage as they develop; some grow like a green bush while others have leaves that are shaded pink to purple. The grower discovers that one variety stands up to the wind but another is laid like broken-strawed barley. He needs to do little cultivating between those rows of potato plants which have prolific foliage and this is of great benefit to the potato as well as being labour-saving.

To come to the actual choice of seed, there are many old favourites. The beginner is well advised to go for these before trying the newest thing in the catalogue for seed is expensive. It takes around three-quarters of a ton to plant the acre. If the grower sprays against blight as he must, and irrigates as he should, he can plough out ten tons or more. He must use the plough to avoid greater damage at harvest time. No digger can do the job with as little loss as a ploughshare. Once lifted the dried potato needs to be stored, and a good keeping variety is the choice. The oldest of the old favourites have been with us for seventy or eighty years. The best of them stand up well to the common scourges of the potato grower's existence. What are classed as early maincrops include King Edward and Majestic. King Edward doesn't do well on light, dry soil, but gives a fair crop on soil with good humus content. It keeps its shape when cooked but is not immune to wart disease although it has some resistance to scab. Majestic on the other hand is immune to wart disease though affected by scab and foliage blight. It gives a high yield on most soils.

In exceptionally favourable circumstances where earlies can be grown, Sharpes Express and Epicure are old favourites, but whether for early or late, the soil must be balanced with farm manure followed by a compound fertilizer supplying nitrogen, phosphate and potash. Advice may be taken on this aspect of soil preparation and where necessary phosphate and potash may be increased in ratio. Planting times will be different according to locality, just as spraying for blight will vary from north to south. Spraying, it must be appreciated, will not prevent blight but only alleviate its effect. The relationship between blight and the maturing of the potato is mitigated to a degree by the time of planting. Potatoes put in early may even have to be irrigated to save them from frost in some areas. Later on, when blight takes its toll, the amount of damage will depend on the stage of maturity the plant has reached. 'Everything in before April is out' is a sound rule so far as the potato crop is concerned. Later on if the crop can be lifted and stored in a well-ventilated shed rather than in a clamp under straight straw, the frost hazard will be avoided and condensation will have less effect should this take place in late autumn through freak changes in temperature. Potatoes being a staple of the English diet, the Ministry of Agriculture and Fisheries supply most of the information a would-be grower may need through pamphlets and bulletins.

Having gone in for the potato, much the same soil condition – good rich loam, well-drained and with plenty of farm manure – will serve a longer-term rhubarb enterprise. Rhubarb planted in November will yield in its second year and is much in demand on the market stall and at the fruiterer's

where the forced type fetches quite a price. The season for other vegetables marches along with the various chores connected with the potato crop. Cauliflower and cabbage seasons run from midsummer to midwinter. There are winter varieties and late-maturing, self-protecting strains of cauliflower and cabbage that stand extremes of temperature.

Care must always be taken in presentation and packing: a few sackfuls of cabbages tumbled out on the floor look like the makings of a compost heap; cauliflowers are easily bruised and disfigured. All vegetables must be gathered and handled with care if they are to compete with the first-class, top-quality product of the professional. Carrots or turnips which are earth-covered may sell to the little shop on the corner where the quality is hardly looked at, but the price paid will be in keeping.

Brussels sprouts are different: gathering them involves the use of many hands so on a small scale they can hardly be worth while. They are at their best after the first good frost and gathering them on a day of sleet and extreme cold is as near to a Siberian experience as any smallholder could contemplate.

Growing salad crops is mainly a summer occupation and offers an altogether more absorbing interest than cultivating potatoes or carrots to be attacked on both sides at once by the carrot fly and the wire worm, never to show a great return. As with most things for which the customer is prepared to pay a better price, salad crops call for more work, raising the plants in a cold frame or seedbox, pricking them out, transplanting and generally caring for them until they reach a prime condition and can be sold. The lettuce should be protected with a cloche to encourage growth and be irrigated to keep it growing. It can bolt if mismanaged and it really needs to be packed and delivered early on a cool morning. The radish grows easily enough but it has to be picked and bundled like the young carrots thinned from the row. Chives are

less of a problem than spring onions, but a chive bed, like a rhubarb plot, needs to be established two years in advance. Where there are cold frames a succession of lettuce plants are brought on and indeed this is one of the secrets of salad cropping, a constant supply so long as there is a demand. The cloche and a polythene cover of one sort or another really keep the salad-grower in business.

Above all the vegetable must be fresh, wholesome and crisp. A flabby lettuce, a wilting spring onion, or a long-dead radish with the blush dying on its cheek will please no one. The man who wants to win in this market must be up early, giving as much time to the preparation of his wares as he devoted to their cultivation. The best seed produces the best plant so there is no point in economizing here. Enterprise in looking for an outlet for your produce will pay off; there are hotels, restaurants and eating houses that will welcome a fresh delivery of newly cut lettuces, freshly pulled radishes and spring onions damp with morning dew. Whatever they may say, people are attracted by the outward appearance; they go for produce that looks good and tastes really fresh.

A longer-term project is growing soft fruit – raspberries, strawberries, loganberries, the cultivated blackberry, and even, perhaps, blackcurrants, a few redcurrants and the dessert gooseberry. As with the salad market, there is a better class of trade where prime fruit may earn a special bonus. The grower needs to think ahead and if he is growing the favourite soft fruits, strawberries and raspberries, he must choose the variety carefully, having once again considered the suitability of the soil for the kind of fruit he has chosen to grow.

Strawberries ripen in the sun but require moisture from the ground and where evaporation is rapid on very light soil the fruit of the plant is never as big as it might be. Rasp-

Cucumbers under glass

berries to a certain extent provide shade to retain moisture in the soil in the same way as the broad leaves of a good strawberry plant will do, but both kinds of fruit are best grown under netting. If they are to be a commercial proposition they need to be caged from the outset. By doing this, 'mobile' pests are kept out. The lesser nuisances can be dealt with by means of repellents, baits and sprays. Virus-free plants are essential and a good nurseryman will supply the stock. There will be an outlay for punnets of the required size, and a certain amount of labour in picking and preparing the fruit for sale.

As with the salad ingredients, the fruit offered should be only the very best. Second grade may go to a shopkeeper who sells fruit as a sideline. When the plants are put in it must be remembered that room is needed not only for the sun to reach the fruit but for cultivation between rows as well as picking the crop. The heartbreak of strawberry growing is a glut when the price barely covers the labour cost of picking let alone cultivation, so that it is wise to grow other fruits which, although they may not be as much in demand, hold their price and hardly ever become a glut on the stall.

Picking and sprigging are the expensive part of growing black- and redcurrants. Dessert gooseberries are rather special but since the gooseberry bush takes a little longer to come into full bearing there is time to find a market – a chef who makes a superb gooseberry fool or crumble, a high class fruit shop where discriminating customers appreciate the very best quality. Taking pains in things of this kind may mean the difference between getting by and going into the red at the bank.

A final word is needed on varieties of soft fruit. As with salads, the best variety to grow is the one that thrives on the soil and gives a good return. Soil and conditions vary and it is wise to take specialist advice on the choice of a variety for a particular district. Once again there is information available through official channels, both on the cultivation of soft fruit and such orchard fruit as apples, pears, plums, etc, which involve a somewhat longer-term investment, even when trees are bought with the prospect of a crop in the first or second year after planting.

Establishing an orchard should really be left to the small-holder with previous experience of fruit-growing. Having decided what variety of dessert or cooking apple he will plant, he must take account of cross-pollinating and self-pollinating varieties and their suitability in his district. Cox's Orange, for instance, doesn't do as well in certain parts of Britain as it does in the south. Golden Delicious may also be a gamble on which local advice must be taken. In addition to this, at planting there is the question of how the orchard may be laid out and whether, even if it lends itself to them, cordons, espaliers, fan-trained, even standards or half-standards are more space-filling than profitable, though on terraced ground for instance, they may be more easily worked with than the bush.

61

Large trees are more trouble when it comes to pruning, spraying and harvesting, but of course they bear a lot more fruit. They need more room for their roots and whatever kind of tree is put in, the soil should be enriched, especially where it is already light, with organic manure. Before and during planting, the tree also needs phosphate and bonemeal. Bonemeal assists the tree's root development, highly important while it establishes itself on new ground.

The question of dessert or cookers is less of a problem with pear trees than apples or plums. In the right district a Victoria plum that bears a good crop, even when its branches need supporting, as they often do, can be quite profitable. The plum, outside those areas renowned for this fruit, Worcestershire and that part of the world, may have its lean years and prove disappointing in spite of ring-barking and root-pruning. While plums need attention when it comes to spraying, the apple orchard always needs care as it develops for if it is badly pruned severe mutilations remain to reproach the man who didn't trouble to consult someone expert at the business.

When such problems are properly tackled and the spraying programme has become a ritual, the crop, particularly the apple crop, presents yet another problem – that of storing. Apples ripen and are ready for harvesting month by month, according to variety. Some are excellent keepers and others have to be marketed fairly quickly. Since apples need to be kept at 4.4° to 7° C (40° to 45° F) in fairly moist conditions, but with free air circulation, not every shed or outhouse will prove ideal for the job. The beginner who doesn't know how to handle pears, which may go sad on him almost overnight, must read the experts on fruit-farming and seek their advice, or market his crop as it is gathered in, which isn't very good business.

Almost everyone with a barn or shed considers, at one time or another, whether there might be money to be made from mushrooms. There is no doubt that there is, but mushroom-growing on a profitable scale is another specialist field: the secrets of success lie in such things as temperature control, compost and so on. However, as a sideline, and given the basic material, mushrooms can be grown without great difficulty.

No mushroom grower can hope to produce the perfect field mushroom: it only grows where the composting fibres of the old pasture are just perfect for the spawn to run. Its flavour when pulled, providing it is not dried, remains with it to add relish to the sauce or a dish of bacon and kidney.

The horsemushroom is a gourmet's dish and since it grows almost invariably on those pastures well dressed with horse manure at different times, it follows that horse manure as a home-produced compost will bring results.

Although there is always the danger of unwanted moulds and spores in the material, and of trouble from pests – flies which thrive in the mushroom bed when it is at the right temperature, and woodlice which have a way of discovering any kind of decomposing and not-too-moist vegetable matter – a stable manure mushroom bed may be set up without too much trouble. Ready-made compost is expensive and almost prohibitively so for anyone except an enthusiastic amateur who has decided to accept the challenge of producing mushrooms for his own table. When using stable manure the temperature of the bed must be regularly checked. The material must always be friable and not wet; any lumps must be broken down and the heap regularly turned over for a week before it is firmly trodden down. It is necessary to make sure that the manure doesn't contain heavy straw and other materials such as bracken or mouldy hay. This having been done before consolidation, at between 24° and 27° C (75° and 80° F), the spawn, which is in brick form, is planted in pieces roughly 5cm(2in) square placed 20cm (8in) apart and at a depth of 5 or 7cm(2 or 3in). The surface of the manure compost is then covered to a depth of 5cm (2in) with finely sieved loam, sufficiently moist to compact when lightly beaten with the flat of the spade. At this stage a covering of straw about 30cm (1ft) in depth is applied and, in a cold district, further protection in the form of sacking or matting is laid on top. When inspection reveals that the spawn has begun to produce, the bed may be lightly watered with lukewarm water, and a little salt or saltpetre will help. The temperature in the building should remain constant, between 13° and 15.5° C (55° and 60° F).

The professional grower harvests with a knife but in this kind of mushroom bed it is best to twist the fungus and remove it from the compost, filling in the hole with a little sieved loam. Replace all the coverings after each picking.

At this stage, two kinds of pest thrive – woodlice and little blackflies that find fungi wherever they grow. A dusting of pepper is useful as a repellent for flies. Woodlice can sometimes be picked off when they have been lured to fragments of apple or apple skin. They are particularly fond of carrots and potatoes which can be used to entice them into old glass jam-jars, etc. Unfortunately there is no really effective dusting powder that won't also contaminate the mushroom as it is being removed from the bed or while the straw covering is being taken off.

Stable compost always has the drawback of naturally decomposing substances – built-in moulds and unwanted spores of lesser fungi. This makes it a far from ideal choice for anyone going in for mushroom-growing in a big way. In this case the would-be grower needs to do some research and seek the advice of those with precise knowledge of the subject. What can be said for the horse-manure compost is that it gives a better flavoured mushroom than that produced in what might be described as sterilized conditions. However, growing mushrooms for the market is not an easy business and most people tend to steer clear of things that are risky.

5
THE USES OF GLASS

It takes more than 'a bit of glass' to make a living out of horti-culture, which is a highly exacting business that calls for an apprenticeship and expert tuition in the growing of crops, plants or flowers. Apart from expertise, capital is also neces-sary. The greenhouse may be either a heated or a cold one; in either case it will be reasonably expensive to buy and main-tain. If the smallholder has purchased his greenhouse or hothouse *in situ* he may decide to use it as a supplement to some other branch of husbandry. Were he to do more than that, he would no longer be a smallholder, he would be a hor-ticulturist, needing considerable technical know-how.

With or without heating, there are many things that may profitably be grown under glass; the list includes pot plants, flowers such as chrysanthemums, carnations and arum lilies, grapes, melons, nectarines, peaches and even figs, as well as the winter strawberry.

In addition to the conventional house there is the 'mobile', used on land wheels to facilitate the cultivation of a new crop on previously unused ground, or to encourage the growth of an existing crop. The mobile is a less permanent structure, subject to more wear and tear; if it is made of plastic, this will need replacing as the 'glazing' disintegrates.

The conventional, static house comes in a variety of shapes and sizes: it may be half-walled, with a wooden structure carrying the glazing bars; it may be down-to-ground-level glazing of 'cottage' style, or sloping sided – a Dutch house.

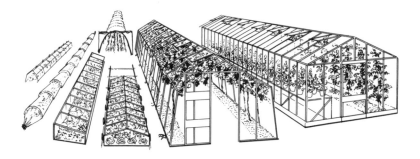

Glass to the ground lets in more light and the perfect vinery, for instance, rises to a peak from ground level when vines are planted with their roots outside the house, the slope facing as much towards the sun as possible. In this kind of structure vines can be laid in due season and raised again after they have been treated. The grape crop, like an orchard crop, will depend on the varieties chosen and whether there is heat or not. The very best Black Hamburgh is as good as, if not better than, most imported grapes but even in the heated house there is a limit to the time scale within which grapes can be grown.

In a less ambitious scheme and leaving the cultivation of the vine for the moment, the greenhouse, whatever its design, can also be used to supplement the work of supplying plants for the market garden from the cold frame. To bring things on, the house will need a propagation section and supplementary heating, if not a system of pipes that are part of a central heating unit.

In selecting a house, the smallholder should choose one that is most easily worked and has good ventilation facilities, room for potting-up and pricking-out seedlings, a water cistern within the house and a piped water supply to it if there is no rainwater drainage from the roof – this is almost perfect providing the stored water can be treated and kept clear and clean. Should the greenhouse enthusiast succumb to one of those soft plastic dome houses that depends on a hot-air blower to keep it afloat, he may also, like a balloonist, need a puncture repair outfit!

Glass is expensive and what supports it is important, so that in buying a house of any design the smallholder has to choose between wood, aluminium or perhaps a precast-concrete structure. Cedar is fashionable and although not the strongest of timbers, lends itself to the installation of fixtures and fittings. Redwood costs less and is very popular. However, both need to be well treated with preservatives against damp and the ultimate effect of this – swelling and warping – which may endanger the glazing. An aluminium house is much stronger. It is less thick, and lets in more light. But one slight drawback, particularly in an exposed position, is that the larger panes of glass are likely to be subject to great pressure in a gale. Once a pane is blown in, the build-up of pressure can easily lift others from the structure.

Concrete houses, with all respect to their manufacturers, can hardly compete with the well designed metal house but one must consider whether there is any profit in do-it-yourself. There may be, if suitable, well-seasoned timber is to be had, and the builder has a reliable plan of construction, but without the best timber the whole idea should be put aside. It is difficult enough to maintain a well-built wooden house if it is treated with preservative or old-fashioned paint without having to contend with structural warping. So much timber sold these days is barely kiln-dried and remains green.

If the greenhouse is suitable for growing vines and the smallholder decides to try his hand at this, an almost automatic choice is the Black Hamburgh variety already mentioned; this is a sweetwater grape, long-tried and greatly relished by people who appreciate its flavour. The Black Hamburgh can be grown in a cold house or in one where the heating can be properly controlled. It is a most attractive grape that grows in a broad-at-the-top bunch with grapes that are oval, in pendulate form and round in circumference. Firm-fleshed and sweet, they are certainly the most popular variety especially in the first crop in August and September.

Hamburghs are not the only sweetwater grapes, of course, and Royal Muscadines do well in a cool vinery requiring something more substantial than a light soil in which they deteriorate in size. As the name suggests the Royal Muscadine has a wonderful muscat flavour and when ripe a very fine amber colour. The Muscat is the choice of the expert and produces very large bunches under the right conditions. Being in the market at the right time is important and if the once greatly favoured Black Alicante grape is now largely out of fashion, though they ripen in October and November, there remain the long-keeping Muscats gathered in November.

While the cultivation of grapes outside the greenhouse may be possible on a limited scale, in the more favourable

Melons growing under glass

climate of the south, of the two systems of cultivation of the vinery employed, one depends on the roots being outside the house while the other requires a root bed to be put down within the vinery. The outside rooting has a distinct advantage in having a natural water supply and a continually refreshed soil which is very important with a fruit of such distinctive flavour as a Muscat or Black Hamburgh.

The vine should be let down in winter and its fibrous, loose bark removed to avoid fungus which is very hard to treat. Although it may be halted for a time by spraying, the whole house and the soil itself need to be cleansed in order to be rid of spores which in due season quickly set off the trouble again. The only remedy for a serious infestation of vines is to cut them back to the root stock, open the place up for a season or more, and let the vines regenerate while the spores die in the ground or wherever they have lodged.

In most cases, only one kind of fruit at a time should be grown in each greenhouse: figs may be grown alongside peaches but not melons – if in doubt it is best to avoid a mixture of crops. The average gardener may overlook the fact that a tomato house requires a different level of humidity from a cucumber house. Melons need a high temperature and a great deal more moisture than tomatoes will tolerate without stem rotting.

Peach and nectarine plantlings are bought in as apple trees are, maiden, two-year-old and three-year-old growth. They may be had from a reputable nursery as two-year-olds, the object being to prune them further to ensure growth for fan-training but specially trained trees can be ordered by someone doubtful of his ability to do this. The three-year-old tree will cost more but make sure that the tree has a healthy, tough bark that is brown rather than green. The difference between a peach and a nectarine is mainly in the skin. The nectarine is said by some people to surpass the peach in flavour every time. There are a number of varieties of both and fruit may be gathered from July, according to variety.

The fan-trained peach or nectarine is grown against a wall and the winter treatment is similar to that of the orchard tree – tar oil wash before the buds have swollen. When the buds develop, syringing with lukewarm water morning and afternoon helps things along. What must be watched is the degree of cold that may enter the house from ventilators left open on a milder day. A good watering of the bed is required rather than more frequent canfuls. Like the hydrangea, the nectarine or peach signals its thirst by drooping foliage and must be given water without delay should this happen. Pollination cannot be left to insects but must be hastened along with the brush or rabbit's tail on a stick. An atomizer aids setting.

Disbudding is necessary when this particular stage of growth is reached and enables the gardener to control not only the number of peaches he would have but also the subsequent development of his tree. In summer the growing peaches have to be sprayed or kept moist by an automatic irrigator providing a mist. Having brought things along through the stoning stage it is best to rig a catch net for fruit that falls. Naturally, the picked fruit has a better flavour than any that falls from the tree.

There is no profit in the cultivation of figs although one may find the occasional outlet for them. Figs thrive best on well-drained ground with a rubble base covered with good loam but no manure. Alternatively they may be grown in a pot and propagated by layering. The plant responds to warmth and watering for its growth and fruit production will be cut short by drought or neglect. In midsummer particularly figs need a generous watering but this must cease when the crop begins to change colour. The fruit is ready for picking when it droops and the stem bends. Figs are more easily picked early in the day and can be packed side by side, in a suitable carton or container. The principal control of the growing tree is disbudding and stopping. A potted-up fig should be stopped when about 60cm (2ft) tall; sideshoots should be similarly stopped until the tree is shaped and fruit is borne on new sideshoots.

Melons have constantly to compete with the import trade. Unlike figs, they require a well-manured bed and in fact the old-fashioned hotbed is best. Seedlings may be raised in pots and established in the bed each at the top of a mound of earth without being too deeply set in the soil. Plants which begin to show signs of canker must be taken out and disposed of and the soil treated with Cheshunt compound if by chance this has been overlooked at the outset. Pollination while there are a number of female flowers at the right stage of development ensures a crop of melons of like size. Four fruits to each plant is what is ultimately aimed at. Once the fruit has set, side shoots must be pinched out as they appear. The stem upon which the fruit develops must not be pinched out but allowed to grow on.

Spraying at the base is as unwise as watering tomato plants heavily at ground level. The water used should be tepid and the treatment given twice every day until flowering takes place. Watering is lessened after the fruit has set and spraying is done frequently while the fruit swells. As with tomatoes, mistakes over watering spoil the fruit and melons starved of water and then watered to compensate will have split skins.

Nets are required to support the fruits on the framework they have been grown against. Keep them on the vine until they are ripe. Their ripeness may be ascertained by pressing the thumb into the end opposite the stalk. When this area is no longer hard but slightly resilient the fruit may be offered for sale.

Strawberries under glass are cultivated to supply the market before the ordinary outdoor crop makes itself available in late June and July. The early spring product is obtained as a result of planning which begins with propagating a healthy stock of a reliable variety. The strawberry lends itself to propagation because of its natural habit of making runners. This the plant will do without encouragement and indeed the whole management of a healthy strawberry business depends on this renewal. The runners are simply pegged down to root themselves and then carefully set in pots to be taken into the greenhouse. Since the aim is to have fruit as early as possible this requires heat and light at a time when the healthy young plant needs this encouragement to bring it first to flower and then to fruit. Conditions similar to those achieved in the peach and nectarine house will suit the indoor strawberry. It will also require pollinating with a brush. Adequate watering and spraying will be necessary until the fruit sets when spraying must be discontinued if mildew is to be avoided.

Plants that have shown an inclination to wilt or remain dormant should be taken out and put with the rubbish out-

side for they can never be revived. This is a luxury trade and it is a fact that the production of luxury crops tends to require heavy expenditure. The commercial grower will be working with mercury vapour lighting and timeswitch controls and will have his luxury strawberry ready for the chef who produces the expensive sweet trolley covered by the *à la carte* menu.

In a less ambitious programme of greenhouse management a more simple set-up may be used for the production of tomatoes, followed up in autumn with chrysanthemums, carnations, and pelargonium cuttings – which sell for a fair price to people who haven't the facility for making them. It is possible to keep florists well supplied with cut flowers from the greenhouse without an elaborate heating system and chrysanthemums are much in demand in the bleak months of winter. The product may not have reached show-bench standard, or have attained the precise degree of perfection it is required to have when a judge's eye first falls upon it, but this doesn't matter. The market wants colour and reasonable size rather than giant blooms.

There are of course, highly decorative chrysanthemums – incurved and reflexive – which will fetch a few pence more than the everyday, common or garden bronze or yellow. The chrysanthemum tends to overawe the beginner and often delights the enthusiast when he discovers that what produces a good bloom is nothing more than care and diligence. Good commercial blooms can be produced without difficulty providing the grower embarks upon his project with good, healthy stock and cultivates it in a healthy house, observing the basic rules to be found in any book on the subject. Since the object is to produce commercial blooms and not to win the silver cup the meticulous care in bringing a plant to have but one bloom is not needed. What is needed is a bloom that

Strawberry plants

will look good in a bouquet or display and will catch the eye of the housewife who wants something to decorate her home.

Plants are obtained by taking cuttings from the stool of the previous year and this stool must not be of old, degenerated stock, but one obtained as a result of buying in reliable plants from the specialist grower whose catalogue will give details of size and the time at which the particular variety comes into bloom. The stools from which the cuttings are obtained will have been cut back after flowering to within 15cm (6in) of the pot level, taken out of the pot and washed before being planted in boxes of potting compost. The compost should be no more than moist and the box rapped to make sure the covering filters down to lie on all of the root. A cool house serves well enough for this purpose and here the stools rest after the exhausting period of flourishing and flowering. From December onwards, according to their classification, stools will be removed from their boxes and planted in the warmed-up house – temperature around 10° C (50° F).

Cuttings will be taken from January through to February, the very latest may be kept as pot plants in due season. Cuttings are taken from the stool and should be robust without being thick or stumpy. A sharp knife is used to cut through the stem of the cutting below the node, leaving a nicely balanced cutting with three or four healthy leaves. A hormone powder helps rooting when the cutting is set in a box or slid down the side of a pot containing a mixture of peat and sand. The sand is important to encourage root development when peat alone might tend to make the cutting rot. A heater may be used to maintain a temperature conducive to rooting without drying out the compost.

From this stage it is a matter of transferring the cutting that has rooted nicely – potting on, first into the 7cm (3in) pot, then into the 12cm (5in) pot in which they may be moved out into the cold frame to be finally brought back in in the 22cm (9in) pots in which they were potted up in midsummer. Bring them indoors at the end of September.

Disbudding is the secret of production. It controls the size and the shape of the plant as well as the number of blooms that are required. On a commercial scale growers shortcut the potting business and plant cuttings directly in a greenhouse bed but whatever method is adopted there is a great deal of work to be done shaping the plant and encouraging bloom, to say nothing of spraying to contend with aphis, leafminer, rust and mildew. Blooms must be carefully tended to avoid damping which occurs in houses that are ill-ventilated and hold cold, moist air. The management of disbudding is well illustrated in most gardening books.

One luxury greenhouse product, which is relied upon by the florist almost as much as the chrysanthemum, is the carnation. Both the heavily scented carnation and the more exotic specimen without scent seem to be quite irresistible between seasons when there is a flush of tulips and a forest of chrysanthemums on the floor of the florist's establishment. The quality of the initial stock is what sets the standard in propagating and producing carnations. Perpetual flowering, the most popular carnations, naturally produce fewer blooms in winter. Given good stock from which to make cuttings it is a simple matter to propagate the chosen varieties, making a cutting of about 10cm (4in) in length by removing the bottom two leaves and setting the cutting in sharp sand after using a rooting compound.

The cuttings are made early in the year with the aid of a little heat and take roughly three weeks to root after which they must be removed from the sand and potted on. Finally they are established in the greenhouse bed at glass level if the house is of Dutch design, or on a built-up bed if the house is walled. The plants should be watered with trickle irrigation and fed with a suitable compound. There is, as always, a shortcut, achieved by buying rooted cuttings for planting in the bed.

6

THE CHICKEN AND THE EGG

However regular the hen may be in producing the egg, there comes a time when it goes off the lay. There is a beginning and an end to the first period of egg-laying and between times things can be managed to the full advantage of the commercial egg-producer by confining the hen, feeding her the perfectly balanced diet, and keeping her in the right temperature and light to maintain output. This can be done nowhere better than in a battery. The hen is expendable. Indeed, it will bring in a further sum of money when sold off to those concerned with the production of chicken-in-the-basket.

The hen battery business may be operated on a modest scale but it needs special equipment, and the battery is comparatively expensive to run on a small scale, so that this kind of business is really not for a smallholder who cannot employ labour and needs to expend his modest resources on more than one kind of husbandry. When the big operators are persuaded to drop the price for a time the small man may go to the wall, and a battery, whether as a result of fluctuation in the market or of disease, can wipe a man out in a very short time unless he has the capital and the insurance to cushion him against such disasters. Even in the battery, where birds are supposed to need few feathers and no legs at all, a time comes when the chicken has to renew its body tissues and its feathers. It will go off the lay naturally. This will happen with more drastic effect when the bird is outside and last longer where it has to recover without being in the warmth of, say, a deep litter house, free of draught. Without doubt the free-range bird is the healthier one, but it cannot be denied that even when it is of a first-class laying strain, it will lay fewer eggs than one living in the luxury of a heated, draught-proof house.

Accepting that this is so, and that the birds are to be kept to produce eggs for sale, the real choice lies between a deep litter house and free range. There is no question that the best possible laying-strain birds must be stocked. These must be bought in, either as chicks or point-of-lay birds, from a certified source. The laying-strain bird, whether on free range or not, is most unlikely to produce chicks even if it could be persuaded to sit. Most of its natural characteristics have been sacrificed in the selection of its strain. It is a laying bird first and foremost. Its going broody, if this should happen, is due to the conditions under which it has been kept, as well, perhaps, as feeding. Both the housing of the bird and its feeding are vital to success in producing eggs and the person who wants to keep a few hens to admire them picking their way across the grass must be content to suffer those shortcomings his lack of attention to details encourage.

To begin with the chicken, rather than the egg, the point-of-lay pullet is expensive. The would-be egg-producer must make up his mind whether he will pay out for the layer or start with day-old chicks. The obvious short-cut to selling eggs may not appeal to everyone. Without buying in the point-of-lay bird there must be some outlay to enable the rearing up of stock to proceed – a brooder, galvanized chick-feeders, water dishes, enclosures of one sort or another. There is no bargain in day-old chicks and it is best to go for a name, a 'brand' of chick (its strain will be elaborated upon in the advertisement) that has been certified and will be delivered, lively, bright-eyed and in perfect condition. The brooder will have to be warmed prior to delivery and the chicks kept in nursery conditions, free of draught and damp until they are feathered.

Losses most frequently suffered in the early stages can be due to the contamination of food dishes and drinkers. Even the floor upon which the brooder may have been set down can hold a source of trouble. Young chicks do have a certain degree of resistance to everyday ills; but the man who would rear them on to become point-of-lay birds cannot afford to ignore basic rules, which, in fact, apply all the way on into the henhouse and the henrun. Hardiness may be cultivated, but abrupt changes of conditions harden off the stock at a price. The transition from brooder to pen and finally to the henhouse should be managed with this in mind.

Day-olds can be purchased early in the year. The early bird catches more than the worm if it is not well-looked after. The keeper of hens takes care that extreme conditions don't affect his small chicks but the birds are vulnerable in damp weather when, later on, they are newly fledged. The fact that they are well clothed doesn't mean that they can retain their body heat when they are penned on a bleak day in spring. The survival rate will depend on how they are handled, but with a sizeable batch of chicks there may be losses in the early days.

To brood the young chicks one has a choice of equipment –

an electric or oil system, or even a simple lash-up of pig lamps over a heavy cardboard carton. The most expensive outfit will perhaps have a thermostat, and there are, of course, brooder incubators, dual-purpose machines that will cope with a setting of at least fifty eggs. The most sophisticated equipment used for chick production will take care of turning and moistening eggs while they are incubated, and all of this strictly under temperature control from beginning to end.

It isn't necessary to go the whole hog in brooding of course. At the extreme a pig-lamp will 'mother' the chicks so long as they are out of the draught on a clean, dry floor in a place where vermin of one sort or another can't get at them, steal their food, or contaminate their dishes. Water dispensers are easily rigged up to supply drinkers. Feeders for day-olds need be no more than the lidded egg box in which a dozen eggs are bought from the shop, the hole through which the chicks will feed being cut in the top-half of the papier mâché carton. Food will later on be supplied by a hopper-feeder which should be hung at just the right height from the floor so that the birds cannot scatter too much of the precious feed, contaminate the feeder by getting their feet into it, or pollute it with their droppings. The cycle of natural parasites is tight enough without encouraging a short-circuit.

From the chick to the chicken means new accommodation and here the whole business becomes a matter of definite choice. Hens may be installed in many different kinds of house and there will always be a lot of work. It is most important that the house be dry, well ventilated, and thoroughly disinfected. It may be fitted with perches and dropping boards or simply with perches. With perches and no dropping boards there has to be a fair depth of good dry litter. This litter will be turned daily and removed long before there is a reek of ammonia. Many people will see a drawback in littering the floor for if only one of the flock goes

off-colour, litter may harbour infection – one or another of the ailments to which the hen is prone. A fair depth of litter – 30cm (1ft) – enables perches to be scraped, but disinfecting must be done regularly with a spray without the turned-over litter becoming too moist. Flies are discouraged in this way.

The litter itself will prove a valuable material for making garden compost. Hen manure, as everyone knows, is much too strong for raw application and needs not only to be weathered a little, but also to be bulked with peat and other vegetable matter before it is suitable for use in the furrow. It is sometimes not a bad thing to use a certain amount of dry peat in henhouse litter when this method is used. Whatever the design of the house it should be high enough to avoid an aching back over the cleaning operation, and admit light enough for inspection without trouble when eggs are collected.

Nest boxes can be of the kind that allow the egg to roll down as the hen leaves the nest. They may be constructed so that they can be emptied from outside the henhouse in which case they must have a reliable means of securing the lid to prevent the eggs being got at by resourceful thieves, human or otherwise. Eggs should be collected and removed to a suitable, cool storing place and the gathering never put off. Eggs that are fouled should be cleaned without delay if they are to look their best. It must be remembered once again, that the free-range egg is cherished because it is supposed to be particularly wholesome. The customer expects it to look fresh from the nest.

The question of whether the egg should be a brown or a white one is hardly debatable. The brown egg pleases the consumer. The 'pedigree' of the chick listed the sort of egg it would eventually produce. A white egg is long out of fashion, though its content is no different from that of the brown-shelled egg, and its yolk just as rich and golden.

A healthy egg from a healthy bird is obtained by feeding the right things – layer pellet, mash, a mixed grain occasionally (though this must not be overdone) and chips, a finer-sized milling a stage between the standard layer pellet and chick crumb. To any of these, vegetable matter, grass, insects, grubs and larvae are the perfect supplement. In the management of the free-range bird, feeding and the daily ration should be as carefully watched as weather changes, for laying can be interrupted not simply by physical disturbance but by over-feeding, especially with grain of any kind. In a rather confined area the supply of vegetable food may be improved by bringing in the residue of the cabbage patch, stalks of broccoli and the like but these, if they are scattered about, will simply be trodden underfoot and contaminated and should whenever possible be tied up so that the hens have to use a certain amount of energy to get at them. The exercise will keep birds healthy and active.

At the same time it may be that over-stocking exhausts the turf and results in the ground becoming sour. The first thing to do is to turn the plot over and to fence off part of it so that it can be 'grazed' later as weeds and grass begin to take over. The over-use of ground, whether for hens or other livestock, is something to be avoided at all costs. When this happens a new area of ground must be provided and the henhouse moved. This is the reason why a certain type of house is designed to be mobile. Movement of the flock will always result in an improvement in the sheen of the head, neck and saddle feathers, and, in due season, will also improve output.

To make certain that egg production is economic it is necessary to carefully measure the daily ration of protein, without which good eggs are not obtainable, and at the same time to keep a record of the performance of individual birds. This may be achieved with a trap-nestbox which holds the bird that entered it to lay. A simple count of the number of eggs satisfies those who believe that near enough is good enough, but an accurate record, backed up by a daily inspection of the flock when it is fed to see the condition of plumage, the redness of wattles, the brightness of the eye, and the condition of the feet and general stance of birds, makes it all much more rewarding.

Hens that are not capable of earning their ration need to be culled without delay. While they may be a little older than the battery candidate for chicken-in-the-basket, they will prove the more tasty bird put in the pot. A very young bird never has the flavour of the mature hen that has laid for a couple of seasons. If this culled bird has a poor laying record she can be improved for the table by being penned and given a special ration. The present day complaint that chicken has lost its flavour is entirely due to the fact that birds brought to the table were killed too soon under the ruthless rule of the broiler business, which supplies the supermarket, deep-freeze and hotel trade, where the flabby, tasteless chicken is camouflaged with wine and ready-made sauces to give it some semblance of flavour.

Is there a hardy breed of fowl that doesn't need so much attention and will yet provide an egg for the table, if not for the commercial market, as well as a little meat from time to time? One might suggest the dwarf hen which was a great favourite with our Victorian ancestors and thrived along with the olden day backyard hen because it was hard to kill. The bantam doesn't lay as many eggs as the larger hen, nor does it lay as big an egg, but it lays a very wholesome egg with a yolk that is probably larger in proportion to white than the standard egg and never as pale as the mass-produced one. There are a great many varieties of bantam. It may surprise some people to learn that, like the ordinary hen, some are rated as layers and some as table birds, though the flesh of the bantam is generally more the colour of that of a wild duck than ordinary chicken meat. Eating a ration of 85g (3oz) of food where the large hen will take 115g (4oz) a day, the dwarf hen lays about a third fewer eggs than the big bird in the course of a year. The Bantam goes off the lay when it comes to the moult at the back end, generally around the last week in September or the middle of October.

The duration of the annual moult depends largely on the weather and the conditions under which the birds live. An open-sided shed with high perches may serve the bantam, for it is capable of surviving in cold conditions, but without doubt it does better in a conventional house. It needs no encouragement to roost out at nights because it is of a jungle strain. Its hardiness derives from this fact. Roosting out, however, it will fall prey to the owl, the carrion crow, the fox, or the rat on occasions, and in the lighter varieties with a tendency to go high at night the only remedy is to clip one wing. Once the stock gets into the habit of going in at night, reversion to roosting in the tree will only occur in summer when the house is perhaps not well-enough ventilated. A house that doesn't have good circulation of air is an unhealthy one, encouraging and inducing broodiness.

The other almost incurable trouble with the dwarf hen is its persistent laying-away and it often happens that the stock is suddenly increased by a hen emerging from the bushes with a train of tiny chicks behind her. Such a bonus is not always welcome when chick meal or crumbs are expensive and the new brood may have to be left to the law of the survival of the fittest.

Not every strain of bantam is prized as a layer, or serves as a 'mini' table bird, for many are ornamental rather than useful. Among the reliable layers are a number of names highly thought of by poultry-men of pre-battery days. These were scaled-down (or perhaps the standard bird was really a scaled-up dwarf?) famous strains such as the Ancona, Minorca, Leghorn. The Welsummer is a most handsome little bantam hen that lays a good egg for her size. Among what might be called the 'little heavies' we have other famous names prized among bantams as both table and general-purpose birds – Sussex, Rhode Islands, Plymouth Rocks, Wyandotes and Orpingtons. Bantams for show, it might be added, are an entirely different proposition and not within the scope of raising a few birds to lay an egg or provide a meal. The show breeder lavishes much care on his penned birds, some of which are highly decorative in appearance and are groomed to appear before the judges in special classes.

While the bantam is a kind of indulgence rather than a business enterprise expected to show a profit, almost everyone who goes in for poultry considers, at one time or another, whether there is anything to be made by rearing turkeys. Like the battery egg, every aspect of profitability of this bird has been gone into and there is no room for the man who doesn't plan most carefully, measuring in-put and out-put, rearing his bird to exactly the right week of its development and delivering it to the butcher or the market when the retailer can get the best possible price for it. It is not that big business has taken over the turkey so much as that the turkey is probably the most difficult bird to rear, subject to infantile ailments and suffering casualties in the first four or five weeks of its existence on a scale probably greater than any other domestically raised stock.

With the young turkey the question of buying day-olds is fraught with much more risk than with ordinary chicks. It is over-simplifying the problem to state that it needs the same well-ventilated, undraughty house and a wholesome litter that must be kept dry but never get dusty. The turkey chick needs more care in those first weeks than the novice may bargain for, and there are bound to be casualties of somewhere between five and ten per cent. The light should be kept on until the young birds have settled and the infra-red lamps raised or lowered according to the reaction of the young stock: these will huddle under them when too cold, and seek the perimeter of the brooding enclosure when too warm.

Buying in poults at six to eight weeks of age avoids losses at this stage but these birds are much more expensive to buy than pullets.

In addition to the problem of when to buy, there is the problem of which breed of bird to choose. Undoubtedly the broad-breasted bronze turkey is the most popular, but a smaller bird, the Beltsville White, is gaining ground because it fits in the oven and suits the smaller family.

The aim of the turkey-rearer, who will have obtained his stock from an accredited hatchery, is to bring his birds to their twentieth or twenty-fifth week, (according to the variety chosen). The very best stock will reach a point where their weight improvement will diminish in spite of their measured food ration. This is the time when they must be killed and marketed. A small-scale project makes it imperative that chicks which have been brought up on starter crumbs (a proprietary brand) are fed on grain, barley, oats or mixed corn supplemented with balancer meal.

The difference between profit and loss will be most apparent in the final stage, not just when the cost of food and labour are taken into account, but when the birds are sold, for they will be delivered plucked and dressed, preferably to a high-class butcher whose customers are discriminating and want a 'local' bird. The scale of the project embarked upon back in late summer will govern the total cost of plucking and making birds oven-ready. Between being housed indoors under lamps and delivered to the butcher the turkeys will have been hardened to the open-sided shed or sheltered enclosure (a walled courtyard or space between outbuildings in which they are enclosed overnight) and tended with care all the way. This is something the smallholder embarks upon with courage and a degree of optimism. Whether he makes money at it or not even the Inland Revenue might not be certain. The 'local farm' turkey is an expensive bird when it has been reared as well as when it is purchased from the poulterer.

7

THE GOOSE AND THE DUCK

The duck is part of the realm of frozen foods; the goose is no longer popular as Christmas fare. So careful planning is needed if either bird is to be worth breeding. An enthusiasm for the Khaki Campbell, the Aylesbury or the slim-line Indian Runner, or for the heavyweight goose of the Embden strain is not enough. It is what the customer wants that counts and the customer may be hard to find.

There are incidental considerations in the case of both species. The best egg-laying duck is not the best table bird, and there is more to the fat goose than the pasture, for at the critical time, when that goose must be carried on to its optimum weight, the pasture has begun to die off. To make the Christmas goose a worthwhile bird it needs supplementary feeding. The heavyweight goose is a long-maturing bird but no matter what breed or strain of bird is chosen, it needs a certain acreage, so many square yards of grass which might have been the grazing for the goat or the sheep, the pony or the calf. A cow won't browse where geese have cropped. Fifty geese will always need an acre of pasture. Only a millionaire could feed geese otherwise. The answer being that if there is pasture enough, a quickly maturing strain of goose may be bought in, brought on in a brooder for the requisite number of days, and then put out to grass. Geese are hardy and ask for nothing better than good grass.

With the smaller or light-heavyweight goose there is another problem. It reaches its optimum weight at an inconvenient time. It needs to be sold as a gosling, so the market must be researched to find an outlet. Even if it is one of the best layers of the domestic goose family, a Chinese, it will only provide between four and five dozen eggs which may sell as omelette material. At top weight, the gander weighs 5.5kg (12lb), the goose 4.5kg (10lb).

The business will be launched by buying in the stock, bringing on goslings obtained through a reliable supplier of fowl specializing in the particular strains chosen. Bearing in mind that it can be expensive to feed the heavyweight, the purchaser may decide to go for a mixed lot and when he brings them through he will use certain birds for building his flock in subsequent seasons. Since the initial stages are the same whether the birds are early maturing and lightweight or heavy birds – Embden or Toulouse – the choice of strains will be given in some detail later.

A haybox with a single lamp will do for half a dozen goslings but beyond this number sufficient heating to cover fifty goslings will be needed and a circular pen should be constructed, indoors of course, with heavy cardboard, a certain amount of hay for insulation on the perimeter and litter such as dry shavings as a floor. The height at which the infra-red or pig lamp is rigged will depend on the general temperature of the building and the pen in which the goslings are deposited as day-olds. At all times the litter must be kept dry. The goslings must never be allowed to become dehydrated so their drinkers must be away from the direct heat of the lamp or lamps. When the birds tend to cluster directly under the lamp the heating is generally inadequate. When they stay out on the perimeter among the hay they are being subjected to too much heat.

They must be fed starter material: hardy though geese may be, their infant nurture is the same as that of the duck or the chicken. They can be housed in an open-sided shed when they are a week to ten days old and will go out permanently to graze with a supplementary feed when they are three to four weeks old. It must be remembered that they need proper pasture. Coarse herbage and sticks and stalks of weeds will not do. They are particularly fond of paddling but the water provided for them to swim in must not be allowed to go sour. In cold weather they use up their store of calories and they cannot put on weight in extreme conditions.

They are also prone to rheumatism and cramp if they are ill-housed, so that however robust the stock appears to be,

they must have accommodation free from draughts or water seepage. Ideally this should be a movable ark of some sort or an outbuilding that can be made secure and allow a floor, part concrete and part dry litter on which the birds can settle for the night. It will be found that the flock goes happily to bed when the house is comfortable and to their liking, but will have to be driven in when the place is cold and wet. When geese have to combat poor living conditions they never do as well as birds that are comfortably housed. The lightweight goose is a Michaelmas bird and will get all it wants from the pasture up to the end of September. The heavyweight needs a grain feed of barley, oats or wheat, or a mixed grain, to bring it on when the grass stops growing and winter sets in. Geese are best fattened in a pen where they may be given a wet mash, grain, balancer meal and greenstuff. This fattening process must be marked down on the debit side, just as the initial ration of starter pellets, wet mash and those supplementary feeds, given in the first two months when the goslings went to grass, all have to be recorded. It must be remembered that a 5.5kg (12lb) goose dresses out at around 3.5kg (8lb). The heavyweight is no exception to the live and dead weight rule and must be raised to its optimum where it will show a proper return. A point is reached where the graph runs down and the goose fails to put on weight in return for food in the same ratio as hitherto. Goose grease may be useful in cookery, but there is a limit to the amount of fat anyone wants or expects from a prime goose!

The goslings bought-in will always be the best choice in the initial stage and since the brooding set-up is very simple the producer may decide to go on this way. The real choice that matters is the bird itself. The champion heavyweight is, of course, the Embden with the Toulouse running second. Both of these take nine months before they are ready for the market. The Embden-Toulouse cross is the most popular bird but there are many crosses with other breeds among the

Embden-Toulouse geese

smaller and earlier maturing strains. Geese are best mated when they are two years old: this governs the initial stocking – they are run one gander to three geese. The smaller geese are always better layers.

The big Embdens are white with bright orange bills. The Toulouse's colouration is rather like that of the wild pink-foot. It has a dark grey head and back. In the lightweights the choice runs to the Roman goose, a most active and very hardy bird that lays well and is sometimes crossed with the Embden as a weight compromise.

The smaller geese, since they reach their optimum weight

much earlier than the heavyweights, are sold as goslings, the Chinese for instance, from when it is eight weeks old. Chinese geese grow to 5.5kg (12lb) male, and 4.5kg (10lb) female. The Roman goose runs to nearly 7kg (15lb) for the gander and 6kg (13lb) female. The Brecon Buff is in the middleweight class: the Embden gander weighs over 14kg (30lb), and the goose just over 9kg (20lb); the Toulouse weighs around 13kg (28lb) and 9kg (20lb); Brecons attain a weight of about 8.5kg (19lb) for a gander and 7kg (16lb) for the goose.

Laying records show the Toulouse and Embden at the bottom of the league with between two and a half and three dozen or so, the Brecon an egg or two more. The Brecon has another small thing in its favour, though its plumage closely resembles that of the Toulouse, it is a comparatively quiet goose. The Chinese goose is a clamorous bird as good as any backyard dog for giving the alarm. The white Chinese is the more handsome of the two strains, white and brown. It lays at least a dozen eggs more than the Roman goose which lays about three and half dozen in a season. The Roman goose is white. All the lesser geese may be bred four geese to a gander.

With heavyweights it is most important not to breed birds before they are two years old or the weight hoped for will not be attained. It must be realized that with the smaller geese the weights obtained are not greatly in excess of a heavyweight duck, the very best Aylesbury. The hardiness of geese, when they are properly housed, and their ability to do well on little more than good pasture, makes them attractive to most people with a hankering to keep them.

The only trouble smallholders may encounter arises, as it so often does in animal husbandry, from over-use of the pasture which may become infested with a parasitic worm. The worm inevitably causes serious weight loss in the gosling and if the presence of the parasite has not been diagnosed before this is noticed, the geese should be moved to fresh pasture and a vet consulted about their early treatment. The worm is not too difficult to overcome but the pasture needs to be rested and turned over.

The keeping of ducks is undoubtedly a little more complicated and requires more personal attention all the way through. Some ducks, lightweights with more than a trace of the wild mallard in their blood line, may need to be discouraged from flying out, though the Aylesbury must remain earthbound for the simple reason that he is not designed for flight. The largest of the ducks and drakes is always a table bird and never a layer. Even the layers show a diminishing return, giving 25 per cent fewer eggs in the second year than they do in the first and so on.

It must be remembered that no bird will lay without the food that makes laying possible. At point-of-lay the layer strain will need an increase in its ration from 225g (8oz) of food a day to 340g (12oz). Although cooked scraps and vegetable matter will form a good part of the ration, a layer mash will need to be added.

What the egg producer is up against is the market and the old story that a duck egg is a source of infection. There can be no denying that the duck egg is more easily contaminated than the egg of a hen, a turkey, or perhaps even a goose. This is because the duck egg has a very porous or open-textured shell which, after a short time, is permeated by whatever wet substance it may come into contact with. Even when it is gathered fresh and clean from the nest, the egg will be tainted if it is, for instance, set down near a peeled onion in a fridge. It goes without saying that cleanliness in the management of ducks, whether they are layers or table birds, is what it takes to succeed.

The ducks will be rewarding because of all fowl they have most character. Nearly all of the strains have a certain serenity about them and this is something to be preserved whether they are to lay or be fattened for market. Where the birds are for the table they will be kept on starter feed for the first few weeks of their life and for the first four or five months in the case of layers. The layers will come into lay at roughly four and a half months and the Khaki Campbell will lay up to three hundred eggs in the first year. As already stated, the second year will show a marked decline and the thing to do is to cull the flock ruthlessly and make table birds of the mature layers, even though a Khaki Campbell provides half the meat of an Aylesbury, reaching its optimum in its twentieth week or thereabouts.

Aylesbury   Khaki Campbell   Indian runner

The essentials of duck housing are that the building should be capable of being made secure against vermin, rats and other intruders such as the fox and other creatures which, although they don't harm the ducks, cause panic among them. A duck goes off the lay all too easily and may be put off its food for two or three days after a serious disturbance.

The house or hut must be weatherproof and draught-proof without being stuffy. A dry house means one that is well-drained and airy, for the paddled-in moisture must not simply be absorbed by the floor litter, but dried out,

96

preferably by the warmth of the sun on the roof. Like the goose, the duck is prone to rheumatism and feet and leg trouble. A lame duck is best put out of its misery for there is no more wretched creature. A permanent house has certain advantages – solidity and regulated drainage as well as a degree of insulation which a lighter structure lacks – but a movable house has a lot to be said for it, especially when it isn't always easy to renew the floor litter and furniture in the darker, colder months of the year.

In the early stages of their life the ducklings will have been housed indoors where they are in no danger of being taken by rats, for rats always have a great liking for the flesh of ducklings. Rat-proofing is easier in a permanent building but it must be remembered that rats can slip in and lurk in corners to emerge when the moment suits them and they are invariably attracted by scents and odours, the smell of mash and cooked scraps. The very odour of duck excrement is associated with food.

When this vulnerable part of the young duck's life is over it will do well enough in the movable duck house which, unless it is custom-built to your own design, will be a converted henhouse of one kind or another. The floor litter should be of whatever kind is readily to hand, but not hay which will harbour mould and hold the wet. Peat, wood shavings, even coarse sawdust from the woodyard will do. The litter should never be harboured for long. It should be turned regularly and shovelled out to a midden before it becomes damp. If enough material can be supplied the ducks will be well insulated and always kept dry by 30cm (12in) or so of wholesome litter.

If the descent from the duckhouse involves a sharp drop the ducks should be saved from the inevitable crash-landing, which may damage their legs and make them lame, by the provision of a gangplank, and the gangplank itself barred with slats every few centimetres to save the birds a slippery ascent on a wet and cold day. A duck needs living space and about 325cm² (3.5ft²) should be allowed per bird, remembering that birds grow.

The open door will allow ducks to come and go but in this case it will mean that certain predators will also have access between opening and closing time. A bit of weldmesh rigged up at the entrance to resemble a trap of some kind serves to keep out not only the magpie and the crow, but also four-legged predators imprinted with the trap because of their thieving ancestry. Beyond the duckhouse lies the run and here it may be wise to contain the fattening heavyweight who is never so active as the busy Indian Runner, and allow the laying ducks and the lighter birds to enjoy free range.

A pond is the perfect outlet for the flock. A stream presents a problem because ducks may swim off up or down water and fall prey to hunting animals of different sorts so that it is necessary to create a duck barrier with wire netting and nine times out of ten this results in flooding. The ducks will enjoy the overflow but not everyone will see it the same way and a pond or large sunken tank is much better. It should be added that the heavy duck will only mate successfully on the water and this is an important consideration where birds can suffer rupture through an unsuccessful coupling. Keeping the pond or sunken tank clean is vital and where water can be pumped in and out or circulation of the pond water achieved by diverting a stream and forming a shallow, gridded outlet, conditions will be altogether healthier. At the extreme an old bath may be sunk in the ground but baths and cisterns can prove very difficult to clean. A pond may be designed with cleaning in mind if an excavation is made and lined with polythene before the concrete is laid.

Aylesbury duckling is best known to the reader of menus. It is no bigger than the dumpy Rouen duck. Drakes of both strains run to 4.5kg (10lb) and the ducks to just under. The Rouen is a bird of finer flavour than the much publicized

Aylesbury. While the plumage of the Aylesbury is as white as driven snow the Rouen is black and white. The duck plumage is the colour of the female mallard. The Aylesbury lays as many eggs as the Rouen, but neither is a prize layer, producing about 100 eggs in the season, where a lesser heavy, the Pekin, running to 4kg (9lb) in the drake and 3.5kg (8lb) in the duck, lays about 25 per cent more. The Welsh Harlequin doesn't take as long as the Rouen (twenty weeks) to mature and is ready for the table at four months. It comes of Khaki Campbell stock and it is not surprising that it can lay up to three times as many eggs as either Aylesbury or Rouen. A cross between the Welsh Harlequin and the Aylesbury – The Walesbury – is one of the most popular birds because of its weight – drakes of 3kg (7lb) – and a high egg-output almost rivalling its progenitors, the Khaki Campbells. The latter bird is, of course, unsurpassed as a layer and comes in two strains, white and dark. Both lay white eggs, and at their average weights, around 2.2kg (5lb) for the drake and 2kg (4½lb) for the duck, are that much greater than the celebrated Indian Runner.

The Runner is also a survivor and the hardiest of the domestic ducks. It lays roughly half as many eggs as the Khaki Campbell. The Runner doesn't need to be confined but it has a foraging habit that is difficult to curb. It constantly turns leaves over and searches through the old dead grass of the orchard, leaving holes such as might have been made by a colony of voles or super mice. The distinctive physical feature of the Runner is its lack of shoulders which makes it look like a schoolboy who is out-growing his strength. The Runner also likes water more than the Khaki Campbell does.

The raising of ducklings, providing eggs are obtained from a reliable source, offers a choice of methods. The eggs may be set under a broody hen or incubated in a small incubator followed by the brooder lamp set-up. To brood, the hen needs to be a bird of ample proportions and one that will sit it out.

Once she discovers that her brood is a particularly active one she may lead them off and they will tend to fall, one after the other, through lack of warmth and the hazards of the variable spring weather, so that a pen as well as a coop will be needed. Ducklings in a netted pen may still manage to paddle and puddle the ground and this will result in casualties at an early age so that it is best to bring everything into a shed and pen the brood there, keeping the litter clean and the food and water uncontaminated as far as possible. The young ducklings will have to be well nourished with starter material. They should not be exposed to other old hens for these will often attack ducklings for no apparent reason, other than their speed, which makes them look like a hurrying rodent – a half-grown rat – particularly when they are dappled.

Proprietary feeds are always expensive for the very good reason that they have been manufactured to provide everything essential to the growth of the particular animal. A table duck is an expensive item to buy and it is almost as costly to raise unless some of the heavy cost of supplementary feeds can be reduced. It takes an expert a couple of months to make a table bird from a duckling and the costing is carefully planned and checked before the price tag is fixed to the bird. In these days when bakeries no longer take back bread the grocer has been unable to sell, it may be possible to obtain this unwanted material. Kitchen waste of many different kinds will do but never feed decomposing material. A sensible approach is to consider what would do at a pinch for a broth and to leave out the unsavoury, indigestible and tough and fibrous material, and pure waste, such as tea-leaves. Slightly frosted potatoes may be boiled up. Carrots that are growing a little old and careworn and so on, all go into the cooking pot. The broth may be improved with a ration of bruised or rolled grain. Always bear in mind that protein is the main requirement where egg production is the goal.

8

KEEPING PIGS

There is a wide difference between raising a couple of weaners for bacon or for the deep-freeze, and pig production on a modest scale. The idea of keeping a few pigs may be appealing – since they feed off cheap food, mainly barley, processed swill, skimmed milk or even whey. On the other hand the would-be pig producer must consider the facilities needed – buildings, a concrete yard, open-sided shed, ready-made pens, hurdles, a strip of pasture and so on. The least compelling reason would be the inheritance of an old, Victorian piggery for these are generally very primitive. It was not known then that the pig's principal drawback is its frequent loss of body heat when it is kennelled at a low temperature in a draughty piggery.

A pig that is badly housed will not make weight. A weaner will hardly live to make young bones if it lives in an enclosure where the trough becomes half-buried in wet and foul litter and the drains don't work because they have become clogged up. Contrary to general opinion, a pig is by nature a clean animal. It may survive in squalor, but colds and chills will take their toll. Ideally, to be brought on as a baconer or to make a fine pork carcass, the animal should be kept under cover in an antiseptic atmosphere and fed a balanced diet which will be weighed, measured, and recorded against the pig's own weight progress as often as the breeder may decide to do this.

It is doubtful if the average smallholder will go in for a brood sow because the sow must be cared for and fed at some expense. Weaners can be bought in, to be kept in either the adapted outhouse or the ark in the field, bearing in mind that no pig can ever do as well on the field as it will indoors. What really lays down the style of operation is the accommodation available and there are many layouts which the would-be pig keeper may consider, providing he has a roof over his head and a place that can be made snug, draught-free and constantly warm while he brings his weaners on.

Insulation is of prime importance, not simply because the heating matters so far as the pig's progress is concerned, but because electricity is expensive and becomes more so. The heat loss factor is a built-in one and a 'pool' of weaners gives off considerable heat which will cause condensation. This in turn, if it does not harm the pigs a great deal, will result in timber rotting and perhaps the contents of bins or other receptacles within the shed or barn being spoilt. An asbestos roof is better than an iron one. Windows in the roof encourage condensation and lights should be in the walls rather than in the roof. The walls are important if the building is other than a brick or stone one and where possible these should be insulated with fibreglass and clad on the inside with cement board. The floor should be concreted with a suitable fall to the drains on either side of a set of zig-zag pens, the doors of which serve as partitions when the weaners are at the troughs or feeder hoppers. There should be an adequate supply of drinking-water and the layout – with kennel gates opening and closing – should allow scraping of the run area. The roof should have a ridge ventilator and if possible an extractor fan should be installed. The only other important item is the heating and the arrangement of infra-red lamps so that they can be raised and lowered above the snugly housed weaners.

The most important thing at ground level, apart from the drainage, is the positive exclusion of draught. This, in an improvised set-up, may be achieved with lagged hurdles or an unbonded structure of breeze blocks, built across the open end of the shed at pig height but removable for access when necessary. The open end of the shed may also be built up with bales to reduce the draught and consequent heat loss. This kind of structure is a step towards the professional's Suffolk type weaner house, and will of course, only be worthwhile where a succession of young weaners are being installed and brought on.

The alternative is to buy in the weaner at eight weeks when it can go out into the field or be housed in an open shed with a roofed pen of bales. These must be well insulated from any source of damp, laid on polythene bags and bound in wire-netting. The protection of the bales against damp prevents them from disintegrating, rotting away and causing the structure to slump. It also discourages the weaners which take a delight in tearing into things and gnawing at woodwork, out of either pure mischief or boredom.

When the young weaners are first taken away from the sow and introduced to a new and strange environment they lose their zest for life. But, after a day or two, they acclimatize themselves and settle down, huddling against one another to make up for being deprived of the sow's comforting warmth. The beauty of the indoor system is that the pigs are not subject to the change in the weather which immediately affects pigs established out of doors in an ark. Ultimately it is a question of the pig becoming acclimatized and perhaps the real difference between one system and the other, given the same feeding and sound accommodation, lies in the length of time that it takes the weaner to adjust to the new life.

At 27kg (60lb) live weight, it may be that the pig has its own central heating well enough adjusted. The weaner shed is a step from the farrowing house and the next move, if there is to be one, will be into the closed yard or the ark on the field. The aim, after all, is to sell the store pigs as pork or baconers. 'It takes a man to breed a pig,' the old hand used to say, 'let the fool fatten it!' The bought-in weaner will be sold at three-and-a-half to four months of age.

Without the arks set on the pasture to be moved as and when necessary, a similar and satisfactory house can be contrived with netted bales and corrugated sheet or thatched hurdles for roofing. Most successful developments in animal

husbandry begin on a small scale so that the first step may be established on a temporary basis with improvised shelter. The arks are really an investment, and go with fencing, a concrete base, and laid-on water. (None of this must be done until the market for stores has been tested and the pig keeper has some experience in buying his weaner and feeding it to make the best weight.)

If even the fencing is considered a too permanent step, pig-mesh being expensive, some saving can be effected by using electric fencing which will serve a turn especially if strip grazing of kale or rape is needed later where sheep are kept. Any do-it-yourself wooden structure of the ark type must take account of the need to clean the house and to move it when necessary, but at the same time the ark must be constructed in such a way that it cannot be rooted up. The troughs provided must also be solidly fixed so that they cannot be overturned. These are points which seem rather obvious sometimes when the pig has shown what it can do with or without a ring in its nose. (Ringing the pig's nose is a comparatively simple operation using the tool for the job. Castration on the other hand is probably best done by someone with experience of this sort of thing though it takes only a few seconds with a sharp knife and a dab of antiseptic.)

The importance of feeding ranks with that of housing and is often related to the breed as well as the season. The early bird may catch the worm but the piglet born in late spring is more forward than the pig born in winter. The size of the litter may also affect the piglet and the weaner if the sow exceeds the norm. Having carried her litter for 114 to 116 days, the sow gives suck to them for 5 or 6 weeks when they will begin to eat solids without much encouragement, early if the sow has had a good milk supply, or late if she has not. The pig that gets the best teat comes on faster, does the same at the trough and outgrows the lesser piglets and weaners as they follow in his tracks.

Weaners bought in at 8 weeks may be taken off to market when they have put on little more than 27kg (60lb) according to their breed. At about four months they go for pork, or make baconers at about 90kg (200lb). Feeding a balanced mix there is no major problem in producing either kind of pig. The proprietary brand is never cheap but it is mixed to contain everything the pig needs to make weight. Mixing the ingredients is a wearisome task and means buying material which must be stored. It is doubtful whether any small operation justifies doing this kind of thing. On the other hand it is a problem to make anything out of the pig unless saving can be achieved by supplementary means. The most important ingredients are barley and wheat middlings, which, like oats, provide roughage. Added to these may be fish or soya meal. The percentages run: 50 per cent barley; 40 per cent wheat middlings; and 10 per cent fishmeal for protein.

There are doubtful alternatives in the form of maize meal or flake and, the small man's standby, swill. Alas for the day of the swill bin, authority has put its foot down and offal must not simply be processed but be seen to be processed. The fishmonger who contributed his tub so readily may no longer do so. This is in the interest of the health of the pig, not to say public health in general. A pig fed on processed swill undoubtedly gets variety and many things not included in the balanced meal. It also gets fat which it doesn't need and sometimes things indigestible, if not harmful to its stomach and bowels. A scoured pig is a nuisance even though it scours because of sloppy feeding and not because it is infected. Pigs become constipated for lack of roughage, just like humans.

For the man who is simply striving to make a penny the pig may have to take what it is given, skim milk and whey, potatoes, the residue of the graded crop boiled up for the purpose, not quite as good as barley by any means, but a substitute to be added to the feed along with roots like beet and swede or

106

mangold. Carrots that aren't exactly marketable are also grist to the mill, but must never be frost damaged; so are natural substances found on the field, grass, acorns, and beech mast in the scrub wood.

It may be necessary to make a change from the haphazard to the particular if the pig doesn't put on weight as hoped. In this case money must be spent on pellets or meal bought from the food depot. Get the pig on the weighing machine in good time or accept the fact that it may have to be kept longer and fed more before it can be taken to market. It is a fact that poor rations result in sickness but the deterioration in the pig's condition may indicate infection. One thing may mask another where there is no regulated feeding programme and no means of knowing why the weaner or the store is not doing well and is actually deteriorating. Putting the ration right is important. Calling the vet is equally important, and he will almost certainly enquire about possible sources of infection.

Having first decided on the way the store or weaner will be raised, outdoors or indoors, the prime question is what kind of pig to keep. There are many breeds, some pork type, some bacon type, many 'dual purpose'. The Welsh breed is among the first of the dual purpose pigs a beginner might consider. It is as hardy as most, but the purchase of a particular breed will depend on what is available in the market locally. The perfect bacon pig is broad in the back and thick and stocky at the hams and the pig chosen may be the Large White which at 90kg (200lb) is about right. The alternative will be a Tamworth or Landrace.

Baconers are slow to mature compared with the pork breed. The real difference between the two at the equivalent weight is that the baconer is likely to have too much bone and not enough meat when the pork pig is just right for market. The pork pig kept on to attain the ideal weight as a baconer will be too fat and the wrong proportions for the bacon factory and the curer. Pigs of many breeds and crosses come

107

between these two ideal classifications and are regarded as suitable for pork and lesser baconers. The Welsh pig has been mentioned, but what it may come down to is price and the breed available locally.

Certainly the beginner must look about for a breed he can most easily rear and make money on, considering that his neighbour does well with this one or that one, and that the big price goes to someone with an ideal set-up with pigs kept under the roof from start to finish. It takes longer to get a return from the bacon pig and there is the important consideration of having to produce lean meat rather than fat. Few people like fat bacon any more than they like fat pork, and the feeding of a bacon pig has to be regulated to ensure that lean meat will result. Unfortunately this cannot be achieved by feeding on alternate days to put on a layer of lean and a layer of fat and producing streaky bacon! The commercial bacon pig is really not for the novice at pig-keeping.

As for the ailments and diseases pigs may suffer from the two most dismaying epidemics fortunately occur very infrequently: these are swine fever and foot and mouth disease. Both come under regulations well advertised by the Ministry of Agriculture. The lesser afflictions arise in the main from feeding and housing. The former can be remedied by the provision of greater comfort, wind shields of one sort or another, and so on. The latter by a change in diet. The off-colour pig is a sorry sight, a sad creature indeed. Having consulted the vet, looked at diet and the effectiveness of the shelter provided, there is little else to be done, except, in the case of contamination, the disinfection of the yard and the kennel.

Milk or dairy by-products greatly encourage the breeding of bacteria. Poor hygiene and lack of attention to food residues, especially the waste from the home kitchen, may be a source of trouble. The rule must be to muck out the yard thoroughly, scrub where possible, use a disinfectant, sprinkle chloride of lime and allow the building or house to dry out

Landrace pigs

completely before readmitting stock housed temporarily elsewhere. This treatment will break the breeding cycle of bacteria infesting the piggery or barn, particularly if the disinfection is accompanied by a thorough scrubbing out with detergent and washing soda in hot water. It may be possible to fumigate but this is something for the specialist who will wear a suitable respirator.

How much of the foregoing information is likely to be of use to the man who wants to keep pigs must be left to his discretion. The pig has to be made to pay. It may be that its destination is intended to be not the market, the local butcher's shop or the bacon factory, but the deep-freeze and home-cure.

This will involve killing the pig and cutting up the carcass for freezing or curing. It is necessary to get hold of a humane killer or to employ an expert to do the job. The novice needs more than a book to kill a pig. Even if he knows exactly where to apply the humane killer and how to bleed the stunned pig, he may be entirely wasteful in his efforts to do what a skilled butcher does so easily. It takes two men to control a pig while it is killed. The use of the pig-sticker knife to penetrate the vital arteries results in the heart pumping out blood which would otherwise remain to spoil the pork. After the hoisted pig has bled the carcass has to be scalded and scraped. The blood having already been collected, remove the offal, wash out the cavity and let the carcass hang until quite cold.

The whole process of jointing and cutting up the pig is likely to be long drawn out by a beginner with only a diagram to show him where the joints are made. Every part of the pig is useful, providing the man who has it butchered likes brawn, trotters, black puddings, lard, to say nothing of sausage, spare ribs and cutlets. A joint may be set on one side for roasting or the liver kept out of the deep freeze, but the remainder will be frozen once suitably packaged.

The bacon pig provides meat of a somewhat different quality having taken longer to mature for bacon purposes. The flitches are cured using one of the recipes for doing this. Bacon is treated with a common salt and saltpetre solution to cleanse it by immersing everything in a bath containing this liquid. The flitches and hams are left to drain and then rubbed thoroughly with the curing mixture – salt and saltpetre with brown sugar, or some other favourite mixture. One essential is that the salt treatment should be carried out where the room temperature is low – a cellar or cold room – because the curing will be affected should the temperature rise during the process of pickling with saltpetre. The salting of bacon is achieved by rubbing in the mixture daily until the meat is thoroughly impregnated. When this has been satisfactorily done, the usual period of treatment covering a month or so, the excess salt should be brushed off and the ham or flitch hung in a dry place where changes in temperature will be minimal. (A muslin cover can be made to protect it.) The old way of smoking ham was to hang the meat in the open chimney over a fire of oak chips for as long as it might take, but an outdoor smokehouse can be constructed with a little imagination, plenty of good burnable oak chips and some sacking kept moist to hold the fumes and maintain the process without heat. Smoking takes as long as salting. It is even more important to store smoked ham in a secure dry place for, cured in this way, it is more likely to suffer the attention of flies and ultimately breed maggots.

Finally, it takes someone with a particular understanding of this highly intelligent animal to get the best out of it. Store pigs are individuals and will be found to have a distinct character. The man who takes the trouble to study them always seems to make more of them. It is unfortunate that when a pig is kept on its own, as it may be when it happened to be the outsider without a teat, it tends to become a pet. Its day of reckoning is then a sad one for the family who have allowed themselves to become too fond of it. There is no way out of this. A pet pig is more pathetic than a pet lamb which, as it grows, can become such a pest that hearts are hardened against it. The lesson is that domestic stock should never be cultivated as pets. The business of rearing for the market or the table must not be put in jeopardy by any kind of sentimental attachment. It is the auctioneer's cheque that matters in the end.

9

THE GOAT AND ITS MILK

The first hurdle in an approach to goat-keeping is surely a willing acceptance of the fact that goats are a tie, for the goat is an animal that has to be milked in most cases, there being very little to be made from it in any other way. There are bonuses or by-products of course, but most people who go in for goats, unless they are full of ambition and have had considerable experience in breeding animals, are content with milk. The average goat sells itself on this alone.

The goat is attractive to some people who imagine it to be a kind of poor man's dogsbody of a creature that will clear up the jungle and munch away for ever in a methodical way depending on its tethering. It is a fact that the goat is an almost omnivorous ruminant. It will browse on the nettle, comfrey, tree-prunings and rough herbage. The man with acres of rough ground will bless it for this. It will not, alas, do very well without a shed or house, left out all the year round. It will do its best with the greenery, but not in the cold months of the year if it is to provide milk and live to a good age.

It has the ability to begin giving milk before it is mated and it will go on giving milk after it has had a kid for two years or more. Accepting the daily chore of milking the goat one might take a leaf from Mrs Beeton and say first buy your goat, for here lies the key to goat husbandry for the beginner. If he purchases anything but a mated goatling he will face problems, both concerned with milk – or the lack of it! That the kid will have to be reared until it is old enough to give milk, either before or after mating, is the obvious drawback to beginning in this way. Even more daunting is failure with an animal that has already had kids and is milking well, for no sooner will this excellent milker be asked to perform for

A Saanen goat and her three-day-old kids

the inexperienced goat-keeper than its record will take a downward turn.

The problem with the goat is its temperament. Goats are individualists and they respond to an individual, particularly the person who has gentled them along and knows how to get milk from them. This was always a characteristic of the cow when it was hand-milked. It remains one of the things about herd animals exploited for their milk. The novice who buys a goat with a good milk record can hardly hope to take it to an unfamiliar place and get milk from it immediately, never having milked goats before. Buying a goatling he will learn to walk before he runs. The seller will provide some evidence of the goatling's ancestry and its mating. Where the milk records of mother or grandmother exist, examination of these will be a fairly reliable guide as to what may be expected from the goatling. It is a matter of preference and pocket whether the goatling is to be of pedigree stock, to establish a small herd in due course along with one or two more goatlings, or simply an animal to provide milk every day. In this case the blood line of the billy to which it is mated hardly matters. The kids will be butchered. Milk will be the objective, but, although the goat will take happily to the rough pasture, some thought will have to be given to its diet, the balance of concentrates necessary to milk output.

The choice of goat is wide and covers the famous Swiss breeds – Saanen and Toggenburg, British crossbreeds, British Alpine, Anglo-Nubian and a fine-boned goat called a Guernsey. The Saanen is noted as a goat that gives a good yield of milk over a long period and is generally a placid animal. It is white in colour, sometimes with black spots on the udder, nose, ears and round the eyes. Those who are dedicated to the breed will say it is the best goat of all. The Toggenburg is a smaller goat, brown-fawn in colour and attractively marked with white stripes between muzzle and eyes, white on legs and hocks and round the tail. It has an average milk yield. Being a smaller animal taking less food, this probably balances out. The British Alpine goat comes of early crosses with the Swiss breeds. Its markings are similar to those of the Toggenburg and like other British crosses it has a better milk yield than the smaller Swiss goat. The Anglo-Nubian is an appealing animal but it tends to be noisy. It will stand extremes of temperature better than other breeds. It has a good butter fat yield but isn't the best milker. Its main facial characteristics are its Roman nose and its lop ears. It is black and white, sometimes roan with black mottling, and it is hornless.

There are many kinds of goats to be had and not all of them, or the people who keep them, would be approved by the British Goat Society who have high standards. The smallholder going in for goat-keeping will therefore do well to seek the advice of the Society, both with regard to stock he may be about to buy, and the accommodation he envisages as adequate for the project. There is no doubt that casual observation leads many people to think that goat-keeping requires no particular skill. Goats are seen in so many places against a wild background that they are considered to be as hardy as the mountain sheep. Wild goats are hardy. They are survivors. They would never yield very much milk if anyone could pen and quieten them long enough to lay hands on them, and they would be found to be the poorest physical specimens of virtually nothing but skin and bone.

Accommodation for goats must be well-ventilated and airy. A stuffy goat house where hay moulds and induces respiratory ailments in the stock must be avoided. The place must be warm, dry and draught-free; and it must provide about 2.2 sq m (24 sq ft) of floor space for each animal. It should include a sleeping platform raised a foot from the floor for it is important to have insulation. It is necessary to provide hay racks in the loosebox area as well as water, since there can never be a good milk supply without water. The water may be provided in a metal or a plastic bucket but the bucket will have to be boxed so that it doesn't get tipped over by the goat, which, of course, is never tethered while it is housed.

In the open, the water supply is also important and a similar arrangement should be made for the tethered goat or goats allowed free range and kept in summer in a straw-bale shed. The goat house or pen will need to have a secure catch, for goats, like pigs, seem to have a way of juggling or rattling things until they open. The weight of the hay rack should be 1.5m (5ft); to prevent waste, since hay is expensive, have a dropping trough or box underneath, so that the odd mouthfuls tugged from the rack and allowed to fall collect in the trough in which concentrates may also be fed along with items of food such as roots.

It is important to keep horned goats in isolation from each other and to have kids disbudded by the vet at the appropriate time. It is also important to see that even during the day goats are kept in if the weather is bad. In addition to the bucket box there may be a milking platform. Not every goat-keeper uses the hinged flap platform, of course, but not every goat stands quietly to be milked, and a routine of this kind is something to be recommended. Goats can be trained as easily as the milking cow is trained and will accept the drill without difficulty. It is certainly better to milk from the side and have the goat under complete control than to struggle after it, milking from behind, running the risk of contamination of the milk supply because the goat kicks or has acquired a restless habit.

Although there is a free-range alternative to keeping the goat tethered there are so many problems involved in free-range management that most people will have no hesitation in deciding to keep the goat on a chain. Free-range means what it says and a goat has no conception of boundaries as laid down in deeds or delineated by hedges, walls and ditches. The browse is always better somewhere else and everyone sooner or later encounters the nomadic goat that has ranged too far. Parts of Scotland and Wales are populated by goats that did this centuries ago. If goats are to browse where they will they need to be enclosed within a sound chain-link perimeter fence 1.4m (4½ft) high. There will still be the problem of bringing them in and milking them. On a tethering peg they will have to be moved at frequent intervals (two or three times a day) especially where the pickings are lean, but the goatling will be all the better for being handled and moved from one place to another.

The alternative to the peg, which may be an iron pin driven into the ground with a heavy hammer, or an auger-type pin that screws into the earth, is a 'line' along which the goat may browse on a short chain. The running tether, a stout length of galvanized wire, will give more freedom than a tethering peg and may be of any length within reason. The line can be put down alongside a hedge so that the goat may

browse on everything that takes its fancy and even stand on its hind legs where it finds something higher than nettles and bankside weeds, many of which provide essential ingredients for goat health and condition. Even the ivied wall provides a nutritious feast for the goat, as it does for sheep, though there is a good reason for keeping a goat away from the plant when it is berried.

Goat's milk is much more easily tainted than cow's milk and will take the flavour of the ivy berry in the same way that a woodpigeon feeding on ivy berries has its flesh tainted. Most things are grist to the goat mill which grinds hedge trees but not, it must be said, privet, rhododendron or laurel which are poisonous. Thistles, dandelions, vetches, cow parsley, hazel and hawthorn, wych elm and chestnut, succulent and fibrous plants that absorb essential minerals, are good things found on the edges of pasture. A tethering peg should be about eighteen inches long and needs to have a swivel ring to take a clip and chain. Swivels at both ends prevent the chain kinking and locking in artificial knots. Where the soil is shallow and there are large rocks or boulders that make stake tethering difficult it may be possible to cover the same ground by a running tether. Whatever method is used, the water bucket must be within reach.

It is a matter of individual preference whether the goat wears a head and neck collar, which resembles the horse's bridle or halter, or a wide neck collar. The tethering chain clip is fixed to the head and neck collar under the muzzle. A goat should never be pulled from the front or dragged into the milking stand but trained to 'walk on' as horses are trained – by being 'led from behind', as the old horse-breakers used to say.

A goat will always produce more milk than its kid, or kids, will need because it has been bred to do so but a goat with a large udder or bag will not be viewed with the same pride as the farmer looks upon a cow with an outsize udder. It can

119

well be that in a season the large udder will be overlarge and drag on the ground. While some of this suggests that the goat is ready to do most things asked of it from its early days, milk supply really depends on feeding. While a goat may feed eagerly in the open it may be reluctant to take concentrates from a bucket or a trough and this may require a little patience while the animal comes to itself and settles down. The goat has four stomachs through which food is processed. The large amount of fibrous food as well as the herbage cropped from the bank and the pasture ensure a good milk supply, being altogether of high protein and mineral value.

It is the goat's capacity to deal with so much material that makes this possible. Anyone who watches a goat discovers that it doesn't spend all of its time doing any particular thing. It browses, it rests, it ruminates, it drinks, meanwhile, it converts the input to output. The richer pasture of the meadow where the prize cow grazes is really no place for the goat but to ensure a continuous supply of good milk the roughage obtained by browsing the hedgeside and the scrub needs to be augmented by at least 1kg (2lb) of concentrate a day. In winter, when an out-of-doors supply has diminished over 2.2kg (5lb) of hay will be needed as a substitute, plus whatever succulent vegetable food may be available from the holding. Particularly fortunate is the goatkeeper with a market garden to provide a residue of cabbage and brassica in general. The 'concentrate' should be a properly balanced recipe. Calf weaner nuts will do. The ration may be fed three or four times a day when the goat's yield is at its best and one feed will be at milking time to encourage the goatling to milk.

It may well be that there is little money to spare for proprietory brand feedstuff; although calf weaner nuts contain the essential vitamins without the goatkeeper having to bother his head about their nutritive merit, what other food may be on hand will have to serve. These items may include coarse milled barley, flaked maize, bran, and soya flour.

There are many other things the goat will eat as part of its daily ration at one time of year or another; for instance, kale, beet, and turnip. However, turnip is notorious for tainting milk and it may be wiser to limit the amount and certainly feed it after milking rather than before. Clearing up the garden will provide browse in the shape of haulms of peas and beans. The kitchen may supply peelings. However, these will rarely be in such quantity as to make much difference to the year's feed bill in which there will be the item of half a ton of hay, although this need not be the best hay, and may contain as many nettles and other weeds as the scythe or the hook may cut down, or things like chicory and sorrel harvested by the rough grass-cutter.

What is most important is that feeding should be regular and never haphazard. A bleating goat is a discontented animal. A contented goat gets on with its task of packing in the material and ruminating. The deficiency in minerals will have to be made up by supplying licks. A lack of iodine, for instance, is evidenced by a roughness of the coat. The milk supply will diminish as the weather becomes colder. It will also diminish if the goat finds its water supply flavoured or tainted so that attention must be paid to the cleansing of drinking vessels.

The problem of seeing the winter through without spending a lot of money on bought-in feedstuff may be solved by making hay and silage, providing the goats have enough room to browse during the summer to allow a certain area to be reserved for foraging and mowing. Here it may be possible to cut the hay with a machine such as the Allenscythe, or to forage in a reasonable way with a heavy-duty, rough grass-cutter providing the green cuttings can be got in without delay, consolidated while they retain their natural moisture by being tramped down or rolled in the silage pit. Both tasks are time-consuming and physically taxing when it may not be possible to gather either crop except by hand-raking it

and either barrowing it to the silage pit or setting it up to dry.
The two methods of using the grass crop are divergent. The
silage won't be silage at all if it lies on the field to bleach in
the sun, nor will it be very manageable as hay put into the
feeding racks.

There are machines for 'hoovering' up roughcut grass and
mowings and they may be adaptable in silage-making which
is not exactly making a compost heap, but a process which
encourages fermentation of the grass and its nutrients by
adding molasses. The silage pit may be brick-walled or have
concrete walls. It must be on well-drained ground and the
bottom of the pit bedded with straw well trodden down
before the foraged material is put in. The forage may be
lucerne or green oats specially grown to be harvested in this
way. It should always be remembered that silage comes
second to hay in food value so that the making of silage will
depend on the work scheme. Grass and other green stuff suitable for the pit can be cut as and when it is available. Hay-
making depends much more on sunshine and a drying wind.
Where it cannot be done with modern farming equipment
but has to be the old-fashioned process of turning the rows,
raking and building into small ricks, it should be embarked
upon at the onset of a dry spell. The silage pit will be successful if the contents are well rolled down and covered over.
When the pit is opened the silage may be cut and fed in the
trough although the goat may at first display a certain reluctance to begin eating it.

Hay-making, when the weather is right, is a matter of getting the freshly cut field dry and letting the air get at the
fibres and stalks upon which the animals will feed in due
course. On a small scale drying may be done most effectively
on wooden racks or pyramids of wood that will allow the
wind to blow through while the sun completes the drying.
The best made hay has a healthy scent that remains with it
all through the winter. It never moulds or becomes matted or

dusty as a result of decomposition and standing-in animals munch it with great satisfaction. This is one of the things the highly mechanized unit has had to forego. No hay hammered through the baler can ever be as good as that made in the old-fashioned way, though only a smallholder may have the time to produce such a crop, and that only because he dared not include the cost of his labour in doing so! Once the hay has been dried and before it is moistened by showers or heavy dews, it should be brought under cover and stored without being trampled too much or packed into a corner where the circulation of air is limited. Kept in this way its nutritional value will be maximum and the goat it is fed to will have a good milk yield.

We bought our goat and housed it in the right sort of house, tethered it to feed, and set it up with a supply of winter rations, all of it directed towards the object of producing milk which, as already mentioned, is largely what keeping goats is

about. The mated goatling will have her kid at the end of a gestation of 150 days, plus or minus ten days at the most. Most goats come regularly into heat and milk supply will depend upon the time of mating. Hand-milking is largely a process of massaging the teat in imitation of the sucking of a calf or kid. The teats are milked after the udder has been wiped clean with a damp cloth and the process should be completed as quickly, and as gently as possible, bearing in mind that the teats and udders of individual animals vary. The flow of milk will decline as the thicker supply is obtained towards the end of the process. Secretion of milk is natural so long as the manipulation of the teat is as natural as can be.

The foremilk will be collected in a small jar or cup and disposed of. This is a precaution that avoids spoiling the rest should milk from one goat be unthinkingly poured into a container holding milk from a neighbour and the supply having blood streaks or some other sign of trouble. Milking, like feeding, should be regular and to the clock as far as possible. Goatsmilk sours easily. It should not be 'over-handled' which means that it should pass from the teat through the strainer and into the can and as soon afterwards when it has cooled, be transferred to the refrigerator. Where there isn't a milk cooler which can be contrived with a bit of hose and a tap at the kitchen sink, milk may be stood in cold water until it cools.

The most important aspect of dairy work is sterilization of all vessels and a high standard of cleanliness in everything to do with the business. It goes without saying that personal cleanliness is involved. Milk vessels really should be of stainless steel and should be scalded. One of the most important things about milking the animal is stripping for where this is not done thoroughly milk yield will be affected but supposing the goat-keeper is a reasonably skilled milker one goat will provide an average of three pints of milk per day throughout the year.

Two goats will supply more milk than the average family could cope with and it then becomes a question of finding a market for excess milk or utilizing it in the manufacture of dairy produce which also means a certain investment in both labour and equipment. The milk may, of course, be stored in the deep freeze, but storing against a day when there may be short supply is hardly what goat-keeping on any scale is about, even if there isn't a fortune to be made from goat's milk cheese, yoghurt, clotted cream or butter.

However, some of these dairy products are marketable, although it may take some time to find suitable outlets. Yoghurt is something of a fad with many people and its production lends itself to the most rich in butterfat supply of goat's milk. It is possible to buy yoghurt culture from manufacturers specializing in it, but there is a simple and cheaper way of embarking on the business – buying a carton of fresh natural yoghurt. The keyword is fresh, of course, for the natural yoghurt is used to prime or innoculate skimmed goat's milk. Once this culture is established it can be kept from day to day so long as no mistake is made in handling the comparatively simple process of yoghurt making.

Yoghurt is made on the stove and the culture thrives at a temperature of 45° C (113° F). At the wrong temperature it will sour and result in an inedible curdled mess that will have to be poured away. At low temperature the process is endangered by the breeding of unwanted cultures that will spoil the taste. Home-produced yoghurt tends to be more runny than the commercial sort, though it is possible to thicken it.

The cream from goat's milk is most easily obtained by leaving the milk to stand in a shallow vessel, a tinned basin, for a day or so, and using a skimmer. The skimmed milk may be used in different ways, to feed a kid if given to it sparingly, to provide part of the pig's feed, or for baking. A cream separator, which is a piece of dairy equipment not in use on the

125

farm very much these days, should be used with care and not when the milk is chilled. Goat's milk cream is not cream-coloured, but white. It whips better than ordinary dairy cream. Like the cow, the goat produces milk with more cream towards the end of summer when the grazing is less succulent. Clotted cream is made by letting the skimmed cream stand for a day or so and then gently simmering it on the stove until it thickens and crusts. The same result can be achieved by standing the cream vessel in a pot of water, letting it simmer and then rapidly cooling the cream which is left for potting the following morning.

There are two kinds of cheese which can be made from goat's milk: soft cheese, which is intended to be eaten within ten days to a fortnight; hard cheese, which is a keeping cheese that needs to be matured before it is fit for eating, is a more difficult proposition and involves using rennet which, in turn, results in whey, a by-product which can be used as pig food. There are many recipes for cheese and they really should be studied in the context of cheese-making as a whole.

It is impossible to deal adequately with the subject of mating and breeding goats when this is something whole books may be devoted to. The question of breeding to increase a herd involves study of the goat or goatling's ancestry and making a choice of the sires available considering on this occasion that the quality of the offspring rather than simply milk yield is to be the governing factor. Drying-off a high production goat means what it says, restricting the water and increasing dry food. Concentrates will be reduced before the expected date of kidding. Some goats give birth standing and some lying down. Occasionally a kid will be ignored at birth and the goat-keeper will have to dry it off and clear its nose and mouth of mucus. The mother will need a warm bran mash after she has given birth but will not be given concentrates for two days and only gradually after that. If necessary, the kid should be encouraged to suck by squeezing milk from the teat on to its nose. It should not be necessary to call the vet so long as the presentation is right, which means that the forefeet precede the head and shoulders.

At about three months the kid will be ready for weaning. This is best done by partitioning goat and kid so that they can see one another. The process is completed over a period by finally allowing only one feed from the nanny a day. By this time the kid will be well accustomed to rough feeding at the trough and the rack, and at six months will be independent. Care must be taken to see that kids are not allowed to bloat themselves on rich grass for this may prove fatal. They should, however, by the time they are grown and ready for mating, have become accustomed to a large intake of bulk food. Male kids will not be allowed to live on because they will need to be castrated. When fully grown they will probably be only of use as dog meat, except for their skins. They should be butchered at three months. The meat will then be just right. It may be used fresh or put into the deep-freeze, and should be treated as lamb.

A final word on the straying, free-range goat. It can be kept in check, if harnessed as the old Welsh shepherds occasionally still harness nomadic ewes, by fixing to its neck a triangle of fairly thick, longish hazel rods firmly lashed together. This 'collar' prevents the animal forcing its way into a gap in the hedge or through a fence and keeps it where it is supposed to be – most of the time!

10

OTHER LIVESTOCK

There are a number of lesser spheres of animal husbandry that may commend themselves to a smallholder with particular facilities suiting or lending themselves to the species under consideration – the rabbit, for instance, mink, pheasants (gamebird or more exotic ornamental birds), fancy fowl or some of the native species of duck like the mallard, pintail pochard or shoveller. Advertisements for a variety of ornamental fowl indicate that there is a reasonable market and that some fowl command a good price.

However, it must not be assumed that these fowl are easily bred and reared. Most of the people in the business have devoted a good part of their lives to the study of particular species and on overcoming the problems of rearing them. In the case of the rabbit, since the object is to produce a meat carcass, a pelt or wool, there can be no question of feeding grass and the sort of thing given to a pet rabbit. It will have to have something better. The breeding of pheasants is also somewhat beset with problems, particularly in the case of birds like the Golden and the Lady Amherst's which, since the source of supply was cut off by the revolution in China, suffer from the effect of inbreeding – the lack of fresh blood. The drawback to the mink is well advertised. It is an escapologist and a veritable Houdini when it is not kept in the right accommodation. It thrives better on a natural, 'wild' diet than it does in captivity, though whether this is always evident in the pelt is not mentioned.

A project to keep and make money from ornamental fowl cannot be launched on the straightforward basis of the existence of a good natural habitat, for a place in which free-flying fowl do well and come and go regularly also harbours predators that live on the eggs and young, and sometimes on the species itself. A bit of marshy ground with the cover of reeds may harbour a great many mallard. A weedy corner of the stream will perhaps be the haunt of wintering teal, but these places have to be adapted to the purpose. The fox, the crow, the water rat and the mink, may prey on stock kept with braced wings: a suitable breeding habitat will have to be created with wire and wood, heavy timber and concrete.

Rearing pheasants calls for a layout of pens, the building of an aviary for the ornamental breeds and some more permanent housing for things like incubators and oil-fired or electric brooders. The work effort necessary here also applies to rabbit production. There is no such thing as overnight success.

Two aspects of rabbit breeding should be considered at the outset. It is quite possible to keep and breed rabbits in outdoor hutches though production of rabbits for a packing station really calls for more concentrated enterprise. The more hutches and sheds there are, the more man hours will be involved in feeding and cleaning as well as maintenance.

Moreover, the rabbit, if its pelt is to be sold, will be best kept out of the sun in an indoor hutch or cage. A rabbit bred for meat will, like the weaner, do much better indoors at an even temperature. Conserved body heat means a better weigh-in and the meat-rabbit is expected to attain its best weight at a little over two months. The building in which rabbits are to be reared needs to be draught-proof and well-ventilated. The temperature should be below that of a weaner shed of course, since the rabbit's heat toleration is limited. With a covering of fur it doesn't suffer the heat loss of the naked piglet and something in the region of 13° C (55° F) will do.

Since it may be necessary to hospitalize individual bucks or does at different times an isolation ward may be set up in addition to the main layout. The cages will either have drop-pings trays or mesh bases allowing droppings to fall through, although this particular facility restricts the use of space, cages of this design not being adaptable in tiers. Top-opening cages, too, are something of limitation for the same reason. Cages are made of weldmesh and the design can be what suits the house best if the rabbit-breeder decides to

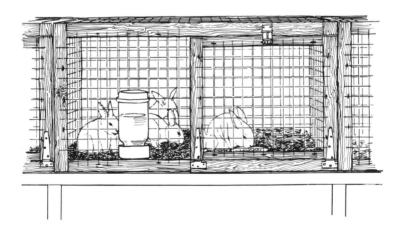

make his own from, say, 14 and 16G mesh. The accommodation needs to be sufficient to house a doe and her growing
litter – roughly 120cm long, 60cm wide and 60cm deep
(4×2×2ft) – and the sides of the cage will have to be blanked
off with an attachable wooden strip in the early stages to
avoid casualties resulting from the young becoming en-
tangled in the mesh or trying to work their way through it.

The decision to breed for wool or for pelt and meat is one
taken at the outset. As with other branches of husbandry it is
best to go slowly and set up a modest pilot scheme in the first
instance. Going in for the packing station rabbit, perhaps
New Zealand or Californian, the ultimate aim will be to
breed something like forty rabbits from a doe in twelve
months, running one buck with half a dozen does. If the
maximum result is to be obtained the only way is to feed pellets. Any kind of manufactured animal food is expensive and
a small scale pilot scheme will produce the basis of costing. It
follows that with pedigree stock the outlay will be greater
than with cheap stock from a local source. When the pilot
scheme has gone through it will be a comparatively easy
matter to work out the cost of investment in a more ambitious project and assess the number of breeding does to be
accommodated. Not every doe or buck will be ideal breeding
stock and for this reason records will be needed so that cul-
ling can be done before things run into the red. The progeny
of the matings will be going out to the packing station at
regular intervals and there will be roughly six litters a year.

Where wool is the end product, and Angoras are kept,
there will be something like 115g ($\frac{1}{4}$lb) of wool to be shorn or
plucked four times in a year and everything will depend on
the quality of the Angoras bought as stock. There will also be
a considerable amount of work, not only keeping the pen or
cage particularly clean and wholesome to avoid matting of
the Angora's fur, but a certain amount of grooming and individual attention not called for by the meat breed. A nesting

area is required by the doe and this may be an insert for the weldmesh cage containing a nesting litter, shavings, hay or straw. It is important that this solid insert, a box open at the top and about half the size of the cage itself, has one side roughly half the height of the other three so that the doe may easily come and go and when she has a mind to, escape the attention of her litter. The doe will be remated as her litter is weaned in the second month. The quickly-maturing packing station breed will be ready for market a week or so after this and will weigh about 2kg (4lb).

It is more than likely that in the early stages of the project the rabbit meat producer will be dismayed at the casualties that occur. Some of these will be due to mismanagement and some, perhaps, to poor stock. If rabbits are kept in conjunction with a market garden there will be a saving in manufactured food and it is even possible when feeding greenstuff to do without a water supply, but greenstuff doesn't always put on much weight, even if the rabbit is a ruminant twice over. When pellets and hay are fed, as they certainly will be in the harder months, water supply is vital and it must not be assumed rabbits can do without it any more than hens can.

The mink has no other product than its pelt, and since a top quality pelt must be aimed at, breeding stock must be looked over before purchase. The mink needs to be seen when it is full-grown, in peak of condition towards the end of the year. At this time the coat is thick. Mink have one litter in a season. They are of the mustela family and related to the ferret and the stoat. In their natural element mink resemble our native polecat in colouration but the cultivated mink has been bred for its skin. Since it is not native to this country those encountered in the wild – feral mink – vary in pelt. Before anyone goes in for mink farming they need to understudy someone already in the business.

The requirements so far as accommodation and premises are concerned are in no way exacting. The mink is a hardy

Six-week-old mink kitts

animal, used to low temperatures and suffering no ill out of doors in cages from which the rain is shed by a sheet covering. The location of the mink farm is all important for mink need to be fed on fish residues and offal. Meat and fish must be obtainable locally and in regular and reliable supply. The second and equally important factor is an ability to skin and cure the pelt. It is possible to skin a mink and leave all the rest to the firm who buys skins in this condition but the price will be affected. The male mink's pelt is much superior to that of the female so that, unlike other sorts of livestock, males are prized over females.

Before there is a litter, however, the mink must be mated. This, as well as dressing and curing the skin, is something best studied with the help of an expert. The female mink is taken to the male and there is a danger of the two reacting aggressively. Gestation takes around sixty days and as with rabbits, a nesting box must be put into the pen. The kitts – nine or ten, if you are lucky and have done something towards this by seeing that the original mating was repeated after an interval of a week – will be weaned at about two months and given full rations to ensure rapid growth.

The bigger the mink, the bigger the pelt. Fish and meat will need to be minced or ground and a certain amount of cereal has to be fed. Essential security beyond the provision of wire cages is a perimeter fence of stout $2\frac{1}{2}$cm (1in) wire mesh set in the ground to prevent the mink from burrowing underneath and rising to a height of four feet. Mink can climb, however, and the top of the fence must be reinforced with a strip of smooth rustproof material to prevent inmates escaping.

The mating of mink takes place early in March and the young mink is ready for market in November when its coat has thickened. This again, is something the expert must be consulted about. A beginner can hardly be expected to judge the condition of mink in his first season. Indeed, it will be some years before the newcomer has served his apprenticeship. Mink are not kept as pets. They are not easily handled and the management of the animal when caged or moved needs to have been demonstrated to the novice before he embarks on mink farming. So too, will the business of killing the mink, when that time comes. Finally, it is necessary to obtain a licence from the Ministry of Agriculture before setting up a mink farm.

The breeding and rearing of pheasants may be considered in two categories: one involves the construction of large netted pens in which the gamebird, a number of pheasant hens run with a cockbird, have cover in which to nest so that eggs can be collected for the incubator or to be set under the broody hen; the other involves setting up a proper aviary in which the species that will live together may move about and have plenty of room to perch and roost. The breeding and rearing are an offshoot and there are divisions in the aviary to accommodate poults and isolated cock birds.

An initial stock of gamebirds can be obtained by buying eggs from a keeper or a pheasantry and bringing these off in the incubator with a suitable brooder to follow up. If there are wild birds on the land, stock may even be obtained by the use of catch-up traps. This will have to be done early in the year and the pen or pens will have to be large enough to let the wild birds settle in the cover the roofed pens have encompassed and become used to being hand fed. The exact size of the pen or pens will depend on the room as well as the money available for buying the material, the timbering and netting from which they are made. It will be necessary to bury up to about 30cm (1ft) of netting to forestall the fox's effort to burrow his way in, and to have a well-fitting door to the pen, even though a determined thief may cut his way in with a pair of snips.

A good supply of eggs will come from as few as half a dozen hens and the eggs will be gathered twice a day and recorded so that the loading of the incubator can proceed as soon as possible. Eggs that are allowed to become chilled by being left out in a frost are no use. Eggs stored can be kept in damp sand. They must be clean and wholesome and all substandard ones rejected. The bigger egg comes as a result of feeding so that a rich protein feed will help things later on when laying is at its peak. A small-scale venture may call for no more than eighteen eggs from each bird during the laying period. A couple of small incubators may be all that is required. The early-laid egg has a lower fertility ratio than the peak-of-the-season egg laid in the last two weeks in April and the first two in May. Eggs going into the incubator need to be of reasonable uniform size, all small and deformed ones having been discarded.

Larger-than-average eggs are put on one side to make a special setting under a broody for the alternative to the incubator is the broody hen. Although broody hens are not found in every hen run they do serve the dual purpose of incubator and brooder. In pheasant-rearing the reluctance of the broody to leave the nest is overcome by tethering her for a while each day so that she can feed and drink while the air gets to the clutch of up to eighteen eggs. A broody of large breed will cover more, but there is a danger of eggs being chilled as the hen 'sorts' them over. When this happens the fertility ratio is bound to be affected. A broody hen can be fed maize and wheat. Later on, when her chicks have hatched and she is penned with them on the grass, she will do better on chick crumbs and high protein feed.

The 'mechanical' brooder can be set up in much the same way as the brooding equipment used for chickens and ducks. Its heating source may be the same sort of infra-red lamp, a paraffin heater, an electric (reflector type), or a gas heater using propane. The shed must be draught-proof. The chicks, supplied with small drinkers and crumb feeders and surrounded with a corrugated cardboard screen, will be given a larger area as they progress by moving the screen outwards while at the same time, the lamp or heater may be raised. The floor will have to be warmed for half a day before the newly-hatched chicks are set under the lamp. The shed or hutch will give access to an enclosed run and in the early stages the chicks will have to be shut back inside the perimeter of the corrugated cardboard each night. However, they will soon pop in and out from the shed to the run by day, and no longer need the enclosure. At this stage food and water will have to be placed outside as well as inside the shed. The run will need to have a top covering to keep out the rain. After about three weeks the young birds will show a tendency to stay out at night and it is wise to see that they are all undercover before dusk with the pop-hole closed. Any disturbance in the course of the night may cause panic and birds driven out into the wet grass or the driving rain may feature on a casualty list. If the early stage of rearing has been done indoors, the young poults will need a gradual transfer to the open pen and will have to be housed in an airy outbuilding that can be netted off and made quite secure from rats and other predators. Once they are hardened, they are ready for the open-air pen at about two months old, when they may be dispatched to fill orders already taken.

In general the rearing of ornamental pheasants follows a similar pattern. The aviary will be not less than 18m (20yd) long and 8m (9yd) wide with 2m (7ft) walls and a roof. The mesh size should be 2.5cm (1in) and 14–16G. A roofed aviary obviates the need to pinion or mutilate the ornamental bird. There must be a draught-proof shelter or hut at one end and, in addition to this storm cover, enough natural cover in the way of shrubs to enable the birds to shelter from the heat of the day as well as to act as windbreak. These shrubs may be cotoneaster, snowberry, hawthorn or rowan. All species of pheasant like cover and additional refuge may be provided by cutting down nearby overgrown shrubbery and laying branches in the run.

Egg-production varies with the breed of bird and there is a small variation in incubation time. The Silver pheasant, which comes from Burma, Cambodia and Vietnam, lays a clutch of four to six reddish brown eggs, but will lay more if the eggs are lifted one by one (no pheasant eggs should be harboured for incubation longer than ten days and the sooner a clutch is gathered and set the better).

It will take twenty-six days to incubate. The Reeves, a magnificent long-tailed bird, and one of the most easily bred fancy pheasants, lays between seven and fourteen eggs of an olive brown colour. These take twenty-four or twenty-five days to incubate. The closely related Golden and Lady Amherst's lay roughly the same number of eggs, between six and a dozen, and take about the same time to incubate – twenty-three days. The Golden lays a white egg and the Amerherst's a creamy white one. Golden pheasant chicks thrive well enough but the fertility of the eggs sometimes proves disappointing and as already mentioned, the quality of the stock has so deteriorated that it is often hard to come by really good well-grown cocks these days.

Breeding birds, and particularly those in less than the prime sheen of condition, require a high protein diet which generally means pellets, balancer pellets to make up for the low protein content of the one-third grain feed of wheat or oats. It may be necessary to include antibiotics in the water supply. Grit should also be in adequate supply. To prevent birds running up and down the sides of pens, as they will do endlessly, it is a good idea to use dividing boards between pens to a height of about 45cm (18in). The breeds recommended above are the hardier ones. Tropical varieties of pheasants need to be protected from frost and cossetted a little with the infra-red lamp in their shed or shelter.

Although some species of pheasant can be run with one another whenever birds are run together they should be

Tufted duck

Mandarin duck

Red crested Pochard

watched for a day or two to prevent trouble. Ornamental birds are expensive to buy and if a battle takes place losses may be heavy. It is usual to run a cock with two hens for breeding purposes. Small clutches may be incubated under a bantam hen.

To expect immediate success and the balance sheet never showing a red figure for the fowl-rearing enterprise is on a par with buying a bull in the local market and expecting to win at Smithfield the next time round. Choosing a suitable holding is the first step, and the right place so far as the raising of duck is concerned, whether they are native species or fancy fowl – the carolina, mandarin, red-crested pochard or magpie tufties – is one with possibilities.

A stretch of river, for instance, is far from ideal. A pond with a gradually sloping bed and a sound bank is much better. An old gravel pit is also worth looking at, for refuges for ducks can be moored out from the bank and nesting places created off shore. In this case, of course, the shoreline may have to be fertilized and pond weed and so on introduced along with flags and perhaps a few shrubs to hold the bank. The main problem may be that the pond is the haunt of rats and other resident predators. Bank erosion is something that a stock of fowl achieve without effort and simply by using the ledge as a roosting or dabbling place, creating an extended shallow in which, as the silt accumulates, they find worms and other items of food. The bank may be reinforced in such vulnerable areas either with built stone or concrete, though it may sometimes be shuttered with timber.

Duck may be raised as domestic duck and are produced or left to reproduce naturally once the nesting sites have been set up. An island is easily constructed by means of oil drums and timber plus a certain amount of compost retained by fine-mesh netting. Nests may be simply small oil drums suitably dressed in straw with one end cut off and litter provided, small barrels cut in half, nesting baskets or even rough-timbered boxes rafted on the pond. Rafting nests are important where the water level may rise after a heavy downpour. Mallard in particular will be quite happy in this kind of environment but they, and whatever other native species – pintail (a more handsome bird than the mallard), pochard or wigeon – will have to be wing-braced or have primary feathers plucked from one wing. The importance of the water refuge is emphasized by the fact that pinioning ducks leaves them at the mercy of a fox that can stalk them in the bank cover. However, bankside cover is of great importance when the ducklings are hatched for they in turn need to escape the attention of predators some of which (gulls) are airborne.

Whether they are raised under a broody, or by the duck that lays the clutch and brings it off in twenty-six to twenty-eight days, the ducklings need a diet of chick crumbs which at about four weeks will begin to be substituted by grower pellets and finally kibbled corn.

Pen-reared birds lend themselves to breeding in close confinement where caught-up wild birds never do, laying infertile eggs. A covered breeding area can only be established where the topography is particularly suitable. Where it may enclose an equal area of bank and water it should be securely fenced and netted all round, with a light roof-net firmly fixed overhead. The landward end will need to be high enough for a man to work under the canopy of the netting roof. The native duck is not as particular as mandarins and carolinas when it comes to a nesting place but these two very handsome foreigners are really tree-nesting birds. In their natural state they would find holes in quite large trees where they would set up house. Unfortunately for the carolina and the mandarin we are short of large woodpeckers and the tree-living animals that leave large holes in which these colourful ducks may nest.

A kind of utility 'tree nest' has to be constructed. This is done by attaching a box or tub to a post or a bankside tree

140

stump a metre or so above ground. A gangplank or ramp will provide access for the pinioned bird which in the ordinary way would fly up to inspect the premises at the onset of the breeding season. The whole set-up may be no more than the roughest carpentry. Where there are several groups of ducks and drakes there will be some competition for the most highly prized sites, and running battles perhaps, but soon the duck will get down to business and begin laying. All species of duck have a secretive approach to nesting and will brood as much out of sight as possible, so that this kind of nesting box should have a small entrance, a pop hole or little more, and room for the duck to literally get down to business in privacy.

While the basic stock may be produced and maintained naturally the person who needs to make a commercial proposition of his wildfowl project will undoubtedly think more about numbers and output. A broody hen can cover fifteen eggs of the mallard and bring them off without trouble. An incubator will give a higher output but it will be necessary to moisten the eggs from the first fortnight until they hatch, especially in the case of the hen brooding in unseasonably dry weather. A hen takes care of the turning of eggs but in the incubator this will have to be done twice a day up until the twenty-fifth day. Eggs should be candled at ten days, however, to avoid disappointment and possible contamination when infertile ones go bad.

Once the ducklings are ready to be penned they will show an interest in the water dish but they are best kept from the swim until they are feathered sufficiently, at about six weeks. Chills and cramp are a bugbear with ducklings penned on rough ground for they tend to get their backs wet in long grass. When the turf is short there is a second drawback arising from the contamination of the ground, so that they must be housed along with their broody hen foster mother, in movable pens. Their water supply requirement is considerable and a hose trickle may be rigged up to accommodate the movable set-up.

The broody hen makes an entirely suitable mother but larger output from the incubator calls for artificial brooding for at least six weeks, after which ducklings may go to the open air enclosure. At this time, since the wings are not developed, ducklings would not be able to flap very far, even in the open, but where the product is intended for the ornamental duck pond or the private lake, and not to stock a shoot where mallard are the requirement, there is a minor operation to be performed while the downy duckling is less than a week old. It is customary to pinion ornamental ducklings in their infancy using nail scissors or a cauterizing tool to remove the outer joint of the wing. This is a bloodless operation and the duckling grows up without this section of wing which would enable it to fly away without hindrance. Pinioning birds at a later stage in life must be done by someone experienced in the operation. Mismanaged and done at the wrong time of the year it can have highly unsatisfactory results, the bird's wing may be infected or even infested with maggots when the wound attracts flies.

The Canada goose is a bird that may be bred by an enthusiast, for this striking species of North American goose has become increasingly popular on lakes here. There are quite large flocks of feral Canadas in different parts of Britain now, all of them escapees from private lakes. People who like to look at the chin-strapped Canada will still buy them if only to pinion and keep them on private water.

The Canada is not a prolific egg-layer, its clutch varying between five and seven. It nests on the bank and breeds without trouble. It may prove itself something of a nuisance, like the farmyard goose, for the gander has a way of defending what he imagines to be his territory and seeing people off, which, to the man who has urgent chores to perform at his duck pens, can be a bit of a nuisance. He also creates slime when he is confined inside a penned area. His principal asset is his contrasting plumage which, when he is well fed, makes him.attractive to anyone who likes to look on a lake with geese paddling majestically from one inlet to another, cocking their heads as other fowl fly round overhead.

11

BEES AND HONEY

Large-scale beekeeping is called bee-farming, not so much because it resembles other forms of husbandry and the care of stock, as for the essential requirement – the farming out of hives. No one can say how many bees can be kept to the acre but obviously there is a limit depending upon the trees and flowering plants in a particular locality. Where there are early flowering plants and the area has more than its share of trees such as sycamore and lime, with orchards to hand, and things like clover and charlock to supplement the early blossom, as many colonies may be set up as a man can manage, but management of more than a dozen will at certain times of the year occupy more hours of the day than a smallholder may be able to spare. It is true that for a good many months the beehives need little attention but, from late spring, through to the end of the summer they require weekly and sometimes daily attention to prevent them from swarming and to see that all goes well and the busy bees have enough room within the hive to look after brood and store away honey and pollen.

A beginner will do well to set up but one colony and learn how to manage it more or less in his leisure time, then increase his colonies gradually to perhaps five in a year or two. This is not quite as easy as it sounds for when learning bee management, even with guidance from a local beekeeper, there are pitfalls, and hopeful expansion is often followed by drastic contraction, if not as a result of mistakes, sometimes from natural causes – a queen being old, damp seeping into a hive and so on.

There are a number of things about setting up that have to be explained in order to avoid disappointment later. The colony purchased as a result of answering an advertisement tends to be a pig in a poke – the queen will rarely be a young one: bees take their pace from the virility or otherwise of the queen, even if they create queen cells themselves and destroy an old queen. The beginner who buys the pig in the poke may at first be delighted to find that he has a swarm – two for the price of one (provided he takes the swarm, knowing enough about bees to detect that a swarm is imminent). Alas, the swarm is obtained at a price for the colony is divided. The young, virile queen stays at home. The old queen goes out, taking stock with her. The swarm will work harder to make stores of course, but depending on the time of the season and whether the honey flow is at its peak or nearly past, neither colony may give very great return for the time and energy expended upon it.

The first precaution to be taken is to make sure the colony is bought and established as soon as weather conditions permit. Someone good at finding the queen should be engaged to do so and to mark her so that her majesty can be located on the brood frames without trouble. Marking will, when the time comes, enable the beekeeper to manipulate his bees, getting rid of the old queen and encouraging the workers to create a new cell or cells so that she can be replaced.

The question of how the bees are to be housed will always be debated by those who favour different designs of hive. The National hive in its simplest terms is a set of 'crates' (or lifts) precisely carpentered to sit one on top of the other, the bottom one being deeper than those that go on top and containing the deeper brood frames. On a full colony there will be one, one and a half (using honey frames) or even two crates of brood frames through which the queen may travel on her endless egg-laying expedition which follows her nuptial flight. On top of these brood crates goes the queen excluder and on top of this as many honey crates containing store frames as the work of the colony justifies being put on.

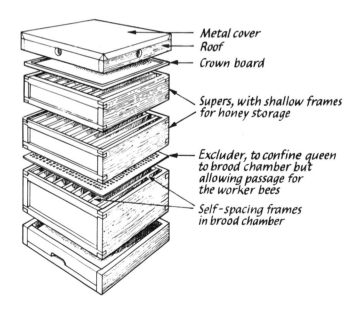

Metal cover
Roof
Crown board

Supers, with shallow frames for honey storage

Excluder, to confine queen to brood chamber but allowing passage for the worker bees

Self-spacing frames in brood chamber

There follows a crown board or a quilt and then the snug and waterproof lid of the hive.

In addition to this type of hive which has a variation known as the Commercial, there are a number of older-fashioned hive designs, the most popular of which is the WBC named after its inventor, W. B. Carr. The WBC hive is heavy and cumbersome. It is not a hive for transporting to the orchard and the moor because of its movable parts, being a double-walled hive. The internal 'furniture' closely resembles the National hive, a series of brood and honey crates with a queen excluder. Housing this stack of crates is the box structure of the hive fashioned in a series of lifts standing on the base or flight board. The beauty of this old hive is that it insulates the bee colony from extremes of heat and cold. It is certainly more reliable in keeping out the rain. Its drawbacks are that if it is home-made or purchased from a supplier it must always be more costly, requiring almost twice as much timber and more work to make it.

Bees may manage well enough independently to keep warm; but their main enemies are damp and draughts. They can never survive when water gets in, so the hive, whatever its type, must be waterproof and, it must be said, airy, for condensation can be almost as dangerous as a leaking roof. Bees will die of a chill, dwindling in numbers until they cannot retain the heat of the brood cluster and this needs to be maintained. It is done in two ways, by ensuring that the soundly constructed hive is sited in a sheltered position – out of the east wind, away from driving rain carried on the prevailing wind, and towards the south or the radius of the sun's travel, and by ensuring that the bees have ample stores to see them through. Bees can't forage in mid winter. There would be nothing for them to bring in if they could and they remain clustering about the queen in the nerve centre of the hive for most of the time, food being tapped from the store cells round about.

The wintering stock should be topped up with sugar syrup or candy but the most important thing in bee management is to see that enough honey is left to bring the colony through to spring. Starvation, funnily enough, doesn't occur in mid-winter but in the gap between winter and mid-spring when the foraging bees, discouraged and unable to venture out after the March wind and the colder days of April, have to fall back on the diminished store. When little is brought in the queen doesn't lay. The brood is small, laying at the maximum rate is delayed and the colony may not be able to make the best of the honey flow. This is what bee management really means, although the beginner will not face all of these problems when he receives his first stock from the supplier in the softer days of mid-April or thereabouts.

Having decided where the bees are best sited, he will have set up his hive on a level base – a flagstone firmly bedded on a bit of ground clear of tall grass and obstructions in the flight line. The next thing to do is to install his bees which arrive in a bee transport box of one sort or another. The best supplier will send a box that at a pinch may be sited where the hive stands for a day or two without the bees being moved out of it. This may be necessary should the weather be unfavourable for the operation. If the hive is a National, the brood chamber will contain two or three frames of brood foundation to make up the space and the bee stores and stock together with adhering bees will be set down in position by balancing the transport box on the top of the hive and carefully lifting each individual frame into place. The purpose of this is that should the queen and her attendants be shaken off, or drop off, they will drop into the hive and not on to the grass outside where the queen may be injured or chilled and subsequently die. This transfer should be done as smoothly and with as little disturbance as possible, the components of the hive put together, and the bees left to settle down.

The same thing applies in the case of the WBC which,

although larger and bulkier, involves less hazard in the process of installing the queen. There is another way of doing the whole thing which involves turning the bee transport on its side for the residue of bees and perhaps the queen to walk up into the hive over a contrived ramp, enabling them to reach brood frames and stores already placed in the hive. However, this is a needless and over-elaborate operation.

The young colony will breed fast, the queen laying over a thousand eggs a day when she gets into her stride at the height of the season, and there is little danger of queen cells maturing or a swarm resulting in the first year. In fact, there would be something wrong if the bees did swarm out. Neither is there any question of contriving increase in this first season. Increase of any kind can only be had at a price for it means the division of the colony, a new queen, a nucleus to be reared and brought along – a business for the more experienced beekeeper.

The most important thing at this early stage of bee-keeping is to be able to recognize the queen and the queen is by nature an elusive insect. She is aided and abetted in this by bees that would cover and protect her, and run with her, concealing her as the beekeeper scans the brood frame, gently turning it when she is not on one side to see whether she has newly trundled over on to the other. The solution is to have the queen found and marked by an expert. She may also be wing-clipped for the same reason that a light goose or a muscovy duck has a wing clipped – to keep her on the premises. When she stays the stock will stay with her. Queens are marked by being given a tiny dab of day-glow paint. This not only lets the beekeeper see that his queen is still alive and well when he wonders about the health of the colony, but enables him to catch the queen and destroy her should she prove to be less fertile than required – or an old queen past her best. The colony will replace her, making queen cells at once providing the old queen is removed before

149

the end of the summer, when they are active enough to replace her.

The natural swarm arises mainly from the beekeeper's neglect and the advent of a swarm is not always detected by someone who doesn't look at his bees every week, which should be the rule in summer, because an overcrowded colony or one with a queen getting on in years will start making queen cells without much provocation. These cells have to be destroyed inside the hatching period of sixteen days. Fortunately they are not difficult to recognize, being single cells the size of a hazel nut, depending from the brood frame on the edge of which they have been specially constructed to be laid in by the queen and fed royal jelly. Destruction of the cells prevents the emergence of a second, third or fourth queen, as the case may be, and the subsequent division and swarm.

Taking the swarm, providing the beekeeper has noticed that things have reached a critical stage, which is evidenced by scout bees going in and out of adjoining empty hives, is an easy business and, unlike all other operations, can be done without beekeeper's veil or gloves. The reason is that swarming bees fill themselves with stores to last while the colony is established in new premises and this may not be for a day or two, even though scouts have been travelling a mile or more in search of accommodation. The first flight is always a short one. The bees, having gathered on a branch or the heart of a bush then move a little farther away, perhaps a flight of two hundred metres. They cluster while they get their bearings, the queen well protected in the middle of the cluster. At this stage all the beekeeper who has observed their flight and knows their location needs to do is to go to them and, using a pair of secateurs, cut the branch upon which they have settled so that it drops as gently as possible into a cardboard box or a nucleus box. Alternatively the bees may be shaken or brushed into the container used. The box is then left on the site, covered with some sacking while the milling throng of disturbed bees rejoins the queen.

In the evening the swarm can be taken back to the apiary and housed properly in a hive ready prepared to receive them. The swarm will generally emerge from the hive after ten o'clock in the morning and before the end of the afternoon on a good bright day. Properly housed it will immediately set about stocking the drawn comb provided, once the bees have got their bearings. No colony will work harder at the business than one taken in late May.

There is no need for the beekeeper to run across country after his bee swarm. Indeed he should reproach himself for ever being in this position. He controls what the queen does or doesn't do and therefore controls swarming. He also controls the business of multiplying his colonies by artificial swarming and does this by dividing his beehive, taking brood cells containing eggs to the top of the hive but keeping the queen down below to lay on frames newly provided. A queen excluder prevents the queen from getting up to cover those frames removed but workers ascending will look after the eggs and larvae they find above the first honey crate. They will almost at once create a queen cell. The date of this cell being developed should be noted. It will not be the usual hazelnut queen cell specially constructed for the purpose but an ordinary cell enlarged in the brood foundation framework. Sixteen days later a queen will be on the way. The beekeeper then removes the lower unit, the old queen, and such workers and nurse bees as are with her to another site, and establishes the new colony down below. The outflying workers and some of the bees that were transported with the removed queen and her brood will return to the hive. The stock strength in both cases will then be adequate for the division. Bees will not desert the queen any more than nurse bees will desert brood they are feeding.

There are many variations in the manipulation of bees.

The one suggested works and the only points to be carefully watched are that a colony is large enough and strong enough to be manipulated in the first place, that the thing is done early enough for both colonies to set themselves up for the winter and that a feed is given as soon as possible after the disturbance, for this ensures that the queen settles down. The same syrup feed should also be given whenever a natural swarm is installed in a hive. Never expect to take honey from the divided colony, though you may get a worthwhile bonus from a natural swarm.

The whole aim of beekeeping is to get honey, hence the Commercial hive and the heavy feeding of bees in autumn and spring by people who are well aware that sugar is no substitute for natural honey, being pure carbohydrate with, as the advertiser would say, nothing added and nothing taken away, although it is quite possible to manufacture pollen and feed this to bees. What you get from a colony of bees depends upon its location and the way the bees work.

It need hardly be said that the best bees are those native to the locality. There are some species of bees that just don't do their best in a colder climate. Israeli bees, for instance, are particularly reluctant to draw the comb unless the temperature is high. A hardy local stock comes from a line of bees that has come through all the hazards of the local climate for generations. It generally produces as much honey as any strain brought in. What is a good return? About twenty pounds of honey per crate would satisfy most beekeepers. Two crates or supers per hive on a colony of a brood to a brood and a half. More in a good season from a strong, double-brooded colony. The figures will vary from season to season as well as from place to place. Every beekeeper will meet the man who has three, four and five crates per hive, a hundredweight to every colony. He may also have encountered the fisherman with extending arms.

The regular inspection of hives in summer serves two

important purposes. It provides an opportunity to inspect the laying range of the queen and to make a decision regarding the movement of brood frames to encourage her to cover a larger area. At least two frames of new brood foundation per brood box should be put in each spring because the size of old brood cells diminishes from over-use. The second important purpose is to watch and regulate accommodation for the honey flow. This in the simplest terms means putting on a super, a simple enough business which doesn't require the use of the standby tool known as a bee-smoker. As cells are filled with honey the hard-working foragers find themselves in need of more comb into which they will put surplus. Bees, whose task is capping, begin to seal cells already filled with ripened honey. They do this after a degree of water evaporation has taken place for this ensures that the honey will keep without beginning to ferment. The steady capping of frames indicates that the now ripe honey will keep. It is therefore ready for harvesting. When the capped crate or super is in this condition it can be whisked away, but if that extra accommodation has not been provided two things may result, the bees may begin building extra comb here, there, and everywhere, gilding between frames and creating a problem for the beekeeper too lazy to inspect them.

At this time it may be that an overcrowded colony with no more room for stores will make arrangements to divide. This is where all may be lost. The hive needs to be supered in good time. This having already been done, the honey is taken by using a clearing board, a board in which is set a bee port or one-way door. Bees coming down from the storehouse cannot ascend again. The board, set in place between the newly filled heavy crate and the queen excluder laying on the brood box, makes certain that when, on the following day, the crate is taken away, there will be few if any bees in the 'sandwich'. This bit of manipulation doesn't really warrant the use of the smoker and, if done at midday when most

of the foragers are out, can be accomplished with little difficulty. The heavy crate is lifted off, covered with a quilt or
blanket and finally transported to a bee-proof shed or building for uncapping and extraction. The hive lid, top super and
other items of hive furniture will of course have to be back in
place before the crate is carried away.

Apart from the hive and its fixtures and fittings bought
from a bee-supplier – do-it-yourself components of brood
frames, shallow frames, metal ends, nails and larger items
such as brood boxes and honey crates for the WBC hive –
there are a number of other items with which the beekeeper
must equip himself. Not the least important of these are the
personal items, a good hive tool for prising the brood boxes
and honey supers apart – the bees bond these together with
propolis – gloves with elastic sleeves, the smoker already
mentioned, and an overall thick enough to withstand attack
(bees can sting through light nylon) and with zip pockets
and a zip from fly to neck.

Old hands may take chances with bees and handle them with a contempt born of familiarity but the beginner who finds himself under attack, having knocked over his hive or committed some other outrage against an already ill-tempered colony, will do well to take every measure to keep bees from his more tender and vulnerable parts! He will tuck his overalls into his wellingtons and make sure bees cannot get down to ascend via his bare legs, and wear a good, firm-brimmed hat to take an ample veil standing well out from his face and neck. Whether the veil is worn over or under the overall doesn't matter; what does matter in the early stages is that the bees can be handled without nervousness, especially when the brood frames are being lifted out for examination and other major manipulations are being attempted. Bees always reflect the nature of the man who handles them and it is certainly a fact that a nervous, jumpy individual always has an aggressive colony. It pays to wear the standard uniform on important occasions such as the honey harvest. Bees that become alarmed will stay that way for several days, and if there is work to be done in adjoining hives the man who doesn't take precautions may be seen off.

Having carried his honey to the house, the harvester then needs to bear in mind that if he has brought in his honey on a warm day he is ideally situated to begin extracting. There being no further need to wear armour, he takes off his veil and gloves and proceeds to uncap each frame, using a series of knives lifted from a large can of boiling water. Some people use a knife with an electric element. The hot knife cuts the capping away, quickly and smoothly. When both sides of the frame have been uncapped it is placed in the extractor. The smaller extractor takes four frames as a rule and is operated manually by turning a handle. The honey is spun out centrifugally, runs down the sides of the drum, and may then be tapped off, via a strainer, into a ripener in which it will stand while air bubbles and accumulated pollen grains rise through it. A certain amount of pollen is always present in strained honey and the sample that wins a prize at the show, whether heavy or thin honey, is always one over which care has been taken when it is tapped from the ripener to be jarred up. Good muslin is not cheap but it is better than nylon.

The production of heather honey is an exception to the general rule because of its heavy nature. Such a thick substance cannot be easily extracted and in fact it is very wasteful to attempt to do so. It is even wasteful to use a honey press because this destroys the wax comb in the process. Most beekeepers prize drawn comb because it saves their bees work. Although heather honey is efficiently handled by a press or, if in small quantities, by simply squeezing it in muslin, the perfect way to present it is in the section, which may be done by slight modification to the make-up of the honey crate.

The National and Commercial hives are the usual kind taken to the heather, for the older pattern of hive, being of many components and double-walled, makes their transportation difficult, the internal parts having to be securely fastened and packing inserted to prevent them from sliding about inside the hive proper, which also has to be lashed together. Where bees have access to the heather, whether their owner intends to have heather honey or not, they will bring it in and this is an advantage so long as the bees have a good enough harvest of ordinary honey which can be separated. The heather honey harvest begins in early August.

If the honey is left in the hive there is little need to bother with feeding, the final care of the beekeeper who closes down his hives for the winter. There are some people who move bees to the heather but are careful not to leave heather honey in the hive when they bring it back because, they say, it tends to loosen the bowels of the bees or affects them adversely when they might have remained in better condition if they had had no heather stores. This is a matter of experience. Bees that work both harvests from the same site are not in any way troubled as a rule. One thing is certain, and that is that bees must either be left with enough honey to see them through to spring, or be well set up with a syrup solution which they can store against a lean time in early months of the year. Feeding a sugar solution is something for the individual beekeeper to decide for himself.

There is a school that insists that bringing a good stock of bees through the winter is easiest done by assessing its size and its need and taking a look at what has been stored. Leave enough and the bees will hardly take down the sugar solution put in on a feeder at the top of the hive. A colony with a lot of room will often take down all that is given and there will be a heavy surplus of sugared honey still in the hive when the bees no longer need any kind of supplementary feed. The commercial producer does his sums and greedily decides that money for honey is what matters. Sugar costs less than top quality honey. He doesn't really care to be reminded that honey is more than sugar and bees may live on carbohydrate just as humans can – only for so long. If all bees needed to keep them going was a sugar ration it would be pointless to leave a gramme of honey in the hive.

The beginner will, of course, follow the book, see that he feeds his stock ready for winter, put on its top quilt or crown board, restrict the hive entrance and generally make things snug for his colony, always bearing in mind the priorities apart from food, a dry hive with a sound roof and nothing within to promote condensation. The queen bee begins to move about to lay much earlier than most beekeepers have in the past thought. Her laying is stimulated by the supply of food and the size of her workforce who will as soon as possible begin to forage. A deprived colony will start late, make less honey than one left well-endowed, and need food the following autumn before the cycle is complete. So much of beekeeping is common sense. So much honey harvesting is greed.

INDEX

Illustrations are indicated by italics

158